D1264402

faith and Education

By the Same Author

SO WE BELIEVE, SO WE PRAY

CHRIST AND MAN'S DILEMMA

PRAYER

THE CHRISTIAN FACT AND MODERN DOUBT

JESUS CAME PREACHING

THE PARABLES OF JESUS

GEORGE ARTHUR BUTTRICK

faith and Education

ABINGDON-COKESBURY PRESS

NEW YORK • NASHVILLE

FAITH AND EDUCATION

Library of Congress Catalog Card Number: 52-5732

SET UP, PRINTED, AND BOUND BY THE PARTHENON PRESS, AT NASHVILLE, TENNESSEE, UNITED STATES OF AMERICA

FOR

GEORGE COOPER HOOD

FRANK GREBE

MONTAGUE WHITE

VICTOR BAER

συνεργοὶ εἰς την Βασιλείαν του Θεοῦ,
οἶτινες ἐγενήθησάν μοι παρηγορία

Foreword

THIS BOOK hardly calls for a foreword: it is itself only a foreword to a vast theme. As for its purpose, it is simply a plea that education shall move in an orbit of worthy faith. Education's pose of "objectivity" may be only a pose, however successful the self-deception; and the man who insists that "we must get at the facts" may easily become a dangerous person; and an education disavowing all assumptions may thereby harbor stultifying assumptions. Perhaps that particular fate has befallen our schools. I have given chapter and verse for the fear.

The human pilgrimage moves by faith. It cannot move by sight, for we cannot see what any tomorrow may bring, least of all the tomorrow of death. Wise men would not change this condition: zest comes by venture into the unknown. If everything were cut and dried, everything would be—cut and dried. If everything were suspended judgment, everything would be suspended. Faith is not make-belief: it is belief, a bright gift hidden in our clay. It comes by the courage of man's will: that is why a credo is the unfurling of a banner rather than an exercise in logic. But faith comes more by the beckonings of God, who has filled the world with signs and come in Christ as "the bright and morning Star." So this little book is a study of assumptions false and true, and of those implicits of human nature which no education should try to escape.

These four chapters are not lectures, but they so began. In original form they were delivered at and for the Centennial Celebration at Austin College, Sherman, Texas. I shall not soon forget the packed civic auditorium and the close attention given to the discussion of a not-too-easy theme. Nor shall I forget the singing of the college choir: "thrilling" would be too contemporaneous and shallow a word, for the music was an enthusiasm (*en theos*) in both excellence and motive. The kindness of the president of the college, Dr. W. B. Guerrant, was characteristic in him, but a grateful memory indeed to a stranger who thus was welcomed as a friend. Appreciation is hereby offered to many other helpers, particularly Mrs. Frank F. Taylor, Jr., and my secretary, Miss Ethel E. King, who typed these pages; and to my wife, who, as in all my attempts at writing, has skillfully prepared the notes.

The threat that darkens over our world may be promise. The word *krisis* in the New Testament Greek hides within its "judgment" the idea of new and piercing sight, and the word for time ("the time is at hand") offers man redemption at the edge of despair. Therefore an age near desolation stands at the gate of life. One heartening sign is the troubled concern of educators for their craft: they suspect that the system is somehow out of joint, and that the wordy generalities now governing them may be sound without substance. The occasional book that voiced such a doubt thirty years ago has become a stream of books. Soon it may grow to a resistless river. These four chapters add their cupful; yet, believe me, not in any disparagement of the teacher's vocation or devotion, but rather in gratitude. Certain teachers have blessed my life, and this book is written in thankfulness. Teachers are culpably underpaid in an age that treasures things more than creative mind. They have labored in a spirit better far than the arid objectivity often required of them. They are benefactors of our pilgrimage, and this book salutes them.

The redemption of education must come from within, but there is a sense in which all citizens are within this endeavor. And—who knows—a voice from the edge of the crowd may help leaders at the center. The best of them are resolved that education shall henceforth move in positive and seminal faith. I hope they may find in this book a handbill distributed in their behalf.

George A. Buttrick

Contents

I. PERSON 13

II. COMMUNITY 44

III. FAILURE 75

IV. DESTINY 107

REFERENCES 132

Chapter One . . . . . . PERSON

EDUCATION, like any other work of hand or mind, is concerned with the meaning of life. This some educators might deny. But if education is not concerned with meaning, it is meaningless and will soon be dead. Every man, teacher and preacher alike, has longed to silence the babel of human voices that he might perchance hear an eternal Voice. If only he could thrust a hand through this moving shadow-show to grasp the Real! A man comparable with a modern college teacher came to Jesus with just that yearning. "One of the scribes," a guide to learning in that time, "came . . . and asked him, Which is the first commandment of all?" [1] The Jews then had 613 commandments, 365 of which were negative ("Thou shalt not"), as many as the days of the year; and 248 positive ("Thou shalt"), as many as the bones of the body. That teacher yearned to know, in longing that was pain, how to gather these scattered flashes of light into one clear beam, as we yearn to bring our confusion of tongues and welter of facts into one sure word. The answer of Jesus was not new, yet He made it new because in Him it was incarnate. "The Lord our God is one Lord: and thou shalt love the Lord thy God with all thy heart, and with all thy soul, and with all thy mind, and with all thy strength: . . . and . . . Thou shalt love thy neighbour as thyself." [2]

I

Education must have purpose, for to disavow purpose would be like disavowing breath; and the purpose of education cannot be different from the purpose of life. It may be more specialized, but it cannot be different in kind. Such a reminder is a platitude, but when platitudes are neglected, they must be underscored. Current definitions of education, even to a sympathetic observer, seem to evade the real questions. We are told that education is preparation for the "good life," [3] but neither the word "good" nor the word "life" is given any content. Or we are told that the "general aim" of education "is only that of pupil growth." [4] But what kind of "growth"? A cancer grows! Or we are told that education must assume "increasing responsibility for participation in projecting ideas of social change." [5] But again we must ask, What kind of change and in what direction? Or we are told that the "crowning responsibility of our education" is to prepare the "young of America" to "discharge wisely and efficiently their political obligations." [6] But what *is* wisdom? And what *is* efficiency? And if education and all who are educated have an obligation, to whom are they obligated? What is the ground, and what is the direction of this strange compulsion?

Current definitions of education at their worst are an intoxication with words;[7] at their average they use such words as "growth" and "change" to advance the definer's own ideas—be he in theory individualist or socialist—as the criterion; at their best they are an unacknowledged borrowing from the Judaeo-Christian tradition. In a recent play, whenever someone said, "Is there anything I can do for you?" the hero would reply, "What do you have in mind?" [8] Somebody should long ago have challenged educators with that question. If instance must be given, this might serve: "I believe that all education proceeds by the participation of the individual in the social consciousness of the race." [9] What does this mean? Anything and everything is the "participation of the individual in the social consciousness of the race." What *kind* of "participation"? What *kind* of "consciousness"? Not gangsterism. Then what *is* the criterion?

The same leader in education has a further baffling definition, this time of faith: "Religious qualities and values, if they are real at all, are not bound up with any item of intellectual assent, not even that of the existence of the God of theism." [10] Notice the "any item": it is apparently quite possible for our race to pledge allegiance without anything to which allegiance is pledged, or at any rate without intellectual assent entering the process. Then he sketches the free man's faith: "I should describe this faith as the unification of the self through allegiance to inclusive ideal ends, which imagination presents to us and to which the human will responds as worthy of controlling our desires and choices."[11] The psychology, then, is as follows: The imagination holds up a rare painting on its auctioneer's stand and, looking across other claimants in the room of personality, says to the will: "Hi, you! This is a good picture. Why don't you bid it in?" The self is unified round the imagination. But what if the imagination should run amuck, as often it does? And *how* does the will know what is "worthy"? Suppose the will doesn't respond? And where in this actual ugly world does imagination find its shining ideals? Or do they come like a magician's rabbit from a hat? Surely education will soon discover that such teaching is a maze—without any exit. Surely teachers will soon turn from this hocus-pocus to the depth and clarity of the Christian creeds, or at least to simple common sense.

To repeat my gentle plea: the aim of education, whatever it may be, is not different from the total purpose of life. A man is a man before and after he goes to college, and he is a man while he is in college. The realm of education may be like a field within a farm: it may cultivate a special crop. But the crop must still serve the purpose of the whole farm. Moreover, if there are implicits behind and within manhood, if there are axioms which human nature cannot flout without disaster, these implicits must govern education. They will take precedence over all other axioms, such as the axioms that govern science or art, because the scientist or artist is first of all a man. The slogan "art for art's sake" has about as much wisdom as "roads for roads' sake."

This truism can be stated in even sharper terms. If God is the sovereign fact for life, God is the sovereign fact for education; and if Christ is God's self-revelation for life, Christ is precisely that for education. The educator cannot ignore God. He can avow faith in God, or deny it, but he can hardly ignore it; for then he would be standing apart from one of the major issues of life and history, and he would be surrendering even his poor experimentalism to a tacit atheism. Nor can the educator be content to let the student add God as an extracurricular according to choice, for again this would be either atheism or the blasphemy which says of God: "Season according to taste." For if God is God, God cannot ever be merely an extra or an avocation. Avowed atheism of some kinds may win admiration, as may an avowed faith in God. But to side-step the central issue, and to try to conduct anything (such as education) as if the central issue did not exist, is evasion. The uneasiness that comes of letting major issues go by default has fallen like mildew on our schools.

As for Jesus, even if He were no more than wise teacher, a claim that most men would allow (plainly He *is* more, for He taught wisdom in an equal love), it would still be appalling that any education should ignore Him. Yet ours ignores Him, and by silence denies Him. In ethics deference is paid to Aristippus and Aristotle among the ancients, to Hobbes and Bentham and Kant in a later time, to Wundt and Höffding and Paulsen nearer our own day, but Jesus is hardly mentioned. Yet He spoke a flamingly original word that has both troubled and shaped our civilization. Let not the reader misconstrue: Jesus is more than teacher of ethic, just as the Bible is far more than "the literature of the Bible." I am here intent only to trace a blind spot in education, hardly distinguishable from the wider darkness. If Christ has any meaning for life, He has meaning for education. Art is for man's sake; and if God is, art is for God's sake. The part, even though the part be education, cannot ignore the whole—at least not without a species of idolatry. At risk of reiteration let this be written again: education cannot live under any hermetic seal, but only under the countersign of man's nature and destiny. If God is, education must live under the acknowledgment of God.

II

But suppose a man does not believe in God? *Avowed* atheism can be, and sometimes is, psychologically explicable or outrightly honest or even brave; but the *covert* or implied atheism that marks education and many another area of modern life hardly deserves respect. Few parents or students would profess: "I do not believe in God." If challenged, they would not subscribe to a godless education. Some men do disbelieve. There are atheists in mind, found in heaviest percentage perhaps in educational circles, though of them it is interesting to note that their disbelief may come from some life situation (from rebellion against coercive parentage or a coercive church, for instance, that professes faith but honors it more "in the breach than in the observance"), as psychology has shown, rather than from *intellectual* bafflement or revolt. Yet because both intellectual revolt and emotional maladjustment gather "reasons," there is some atheism of mind. There is much more atheism of practice. Its name is legion, yet it secretly knows its intransigence. How much *veritable* disbelief there may be—veritable as against psychological or disobedient—is a nice question; for God hides Himself under many names, that He may guide men by His eye rather than by His lash. The atheist's fierce insistence on truth, for example, is plainly a kind of religion—and God is truth. Moreover the atheist's truth rules him. It is far more than a formula on a page. Is it then a sovereign and personal constraint, God under another name?

The stress here being made is that most people believe in God and that they actually do not wish a godless education. Russia pretends to a godlessness, yet constantly accuses other nations of breach of faith; and faith in that connection means, if it means anything at all, a sanction which all men and nations must obey. The botanist says "the purpose of pollen is," and the biologist says "the purpose of marriage is," for no scientist can escape the word "purpose" any more than he can escape other shining words such as order or beauty; but purpose implies, however dimly, personal will, or it becomes meaningless. Education may try to pin to "facts" as though there were no ultimate reference, but the ultimate reference is there even though it may rarely be explicit. Every road sign, though it may seem only a "fact," is governed by a magnetic north. The attempt to deny ultimates brings to mind the story of two boys lying on their backs in a meadow. One said, "There ain't no sky," and the other answered, "Then what is it that ain't?"

This denial of ultimate standards is the reason why our world has reached a "time disconsolate." For houses collapse when built off that vertical line which is stretched, however mysteriously, between the seen earth and an unseen heaven. Right and wrong *are* relative, as our glib age has been quick to assert, for all finite thinking is infected with relativity; but right and wrong are not *merely* relative. East and west are relative on this minor revolving planet of a minor rushing sun; but if a man says he is going east when he is going west, that man is still a liar. And the man can "stand above" his lie to know it for a lie. There is always an axiomatic line in man's life. Conscience abides, and as long as conscience breaks custom, which is what happens in the conscience of a saint, it can never be dismissed as *mere* custom. It may be entangled with custom and therefore need both training and experience, but it has at its heart an inviolable axiom. A counterfeiter or a man who knowingly sells adulterated food is building off the vertical, and his house will fall; for that mysterious line, seemingly flimsier than air, is yet the steel girding of our world. Science is impossible without that bond of honor: there are blood-stained judgments for all men to see. Education also must obey. But why speak of an inviolable vertical? There is a more kindling account: "Thou shalt love the Lord thy God; . . . and thy neighbour as thyself." Is there really any disbelief? Or is alleged disbelief only reversed or inarticulate faith? God is hidden under many names, but He is sovereign fact by whatever name both for education and for life.

III

If someone should retort that education must not make prior assumptions, the answer is clear and instant: education cannot help making prior assumptions. Life itself dictates the necessity that we live by some faith. Recent education has almost deified an attitude of suspended judgment, blind to the fact that while suspended judgment may be possible in matters of opinion or unfinished scientific research, it is not possible on any deeper level of life. We may suspend judgment about the possibility of life on some other planet, or about the cause of the sudden inroad of lamprey eels in Lake Michigan; but we cannot suspend judgment on whether to steal or be honest, or on whether man is a mechanism or a soul. "The sun also rises," and tomorrow we must treat our neighbors either as mechanisms or as persons. The cult of "objective study" likewise cannot stand scrutiny. There is a transcendent mind in man, but also a discursive mind, and in this world the two are joined. No man can escape the pain of that paradox, or leap out of life to survey the cosmos "objectively" as though he were a seraph. As a matter of fact, reason is not neutral [12] as modern educators have assumed. American reason during the last few decades has been individualistic, dominantly scientific, cocksure, and "efficient"—that is, manifestly colored by the American scene. The most comic assumption of education is the assumption that it makes no assumptions.

Every man makes assumptions: he cannot help himself. Thus Huxley's dictum that "theology claims that the just shall live by faith: science says the just shall live by verification" [13] is hardly short of nonsense. For science *in the original instance* does not live by verification, but by faith; and, like religion, it tests that faith in life. Science *assumes* that the universe is one, trustworthy, and capable of being understood by man's mind.[14] That is a sweeping faith. In science also "the just shall live by faith";[15] or, as a more accurate translation of that famous truth would have it, those who are justified by faith shall live. George Santayana has recognized "the brute necessity of believing in something so long as life lasts," yet adds that this necessity "does not justify any belief in particular." [16] But why not? Is there any general truth anywhere that does not find expression in particularity? And why "*brute* necessity"? Why not Divine necessity? Every man must choose some faith. The soundest faith is presumably that which first chooses him. "Thou shalt love the Lord thy God . . . and . . . thy neighbour as thyself."

Let us uncover the hidden assumptions of an education that has posed as a dispassionate and impartial "quest for truth." It has made an assumption about God, namely, that if He exists, He can be ignored. It has made an assumption about Christ, namely, that if He lived and was any better than one more man making one more guess, He does not greatly matter. Thus education, while protesting (with due cause) against "religious indoctrination," has itself been guilty, by silence (a most potent weapon), of *atheistic indoctrination.* It is some comfort to remember that these hidden assumptions of education are negative and thus partly robbed of force.

But education has made *positive* assumptions about human nature, and it is *this* implicit faith which the tragedy of our times has put to shame. The mockery is so complete that the whole foundation of our education must now be questioned. For education has assumed that human nature is a receptacle for "facts," and that this diet of facts will of itself somehow lead to knowledge, and that knowledge by an even more mysterious alchemy will then become wisdom. How much evidence can be found for such a faith? Education has assumed that man is a reasonable creature who when trained in reason can be trusted to act reasonably—an assumption which Freud rightly questioned, and which Hitler's Germany has blown away in a shattering explosion. Education has pinned its faith to a fictitious "progress," blandly believing that man is a romantic creature destined to walk the road of evolution "more and more unto the perfect day." [17] Every tenet of this creed has been falsified: progress has become a rather nasty mixture of cash and gadgets, and the road of evolution has reached—Buchenwald!

The church cannot sit in judgment: it has harbored the same false optimism and pride. But this fact should not make us unaware that education, disavowing worship for "objective fact," has sold out to a grotesque self-worship—the worship of its own analytic mind. It need not surprise us that man, thus pretending to be the end of the universe, fell from his throne—fell into such darkness that he now proposes that "impartial mind" is perhaps no more than chemistry, and that "standards" are only relative—relative being another name for "Chaos and old Night." [18] Surely the time has come, in both church and school, to repent. That word means a rightabout-face, with regret for the past but trust in God for the future. Education is already beginning to bring forth the fruits of repentance, perhaps as quickly as the church. The revisions in college curriculum, from the elective to the required, from overspecialization to a central core of studies, from the technical to the humanities, are an augury. There is hope also in "departments of religion" and in the student interest in them, even though true religion cannot be pushed off into a department. But these moves are only beginnings. Church and school alike must make a new commitment. For some kind of faith is inescapable, and true faith is that which man cannot escape.

IV

Therefore we turn to the Great Commandment. Is this the true faith? To be specific, can "love" be commanded? Three words for love stand out in the Greek of New Testament times. *Eros* [19] is sexual love, in a worthy and radiant sense, despite the fact that the adjective "erotic" is derived from it. *Philia*[20] is the love that binds friends and kindred, again worthily, for without it our planet would be dark. But the word used in the Great Commandment is neither *eros* nor *philia*, but *agape*. This later word, by New Testament understanding, is not earthborn. It is God's love made manifest in Jesus Christ, and then man's use of that gift toward God and his neighbors. *Agape* is a Promethean fire, which glows in the worship of God and in neighborly good will. The Commandment requires that we live in *agape* with those to whom we are bound in *eros,* or sexual love will become erotic; and with those to whom we are bound in *philia*, or friendship will become either sentimental or incapable of bearing life's strain. The demand of *agape* is not that we "love everybody" in a saccharine pretense, for any realist knows that he cannot thus love human nature, but that we hold in *agape* (a word which has the disciplines of holiness and the persistence of devotion) even those whom we do not like.

But can such love be commanded? Yes, for life is

filled with commands which we cannot evade, but which nevertheless we delight to obey. Life points to the fields and bids us cultivate them or starve, yet many a man finds joy in a farm. The weary body commands us to sleep and brooks no denial, but most people are so glad to obey that they "hate to get up in the morning." Why should we assume that obedience is always misery? Whether love can be commanded depends on what is commanded and on the nature of the one who commands. If the doctor prescribes penicillin for our pneumonia, we would be fools to refuse him on the ground that his procedure is not democratic; or if a judge in mercy were to open the prison cell with command to the prisoner to "act like a good citizen," the liberated man could hardly claim that the command is coercion. How would we expect Jesus to speak? By any test He died for men, and in dying love bade us "love the Lord thy God . . . and . . . thy neighbour as thyself." Would we expect Him to whine and plead, or to cast doubt on the wisdom of His own dying love? Such weakness would have left us in frustration. We would expect Him to command: "Now *you* live in love." He does not truckle, any more than the tides. He does not apologize, any more than the stars. There is no democracy between God and man. That is why there can be democracy between man and man. Freedom of the ocean is possible only under the sovereignty of stars.

The love of God, at first His gift and then man's response, is better than democratic: it is constitutional. Only dimly we trace it in the unfoldings of history, only fitfully we see it in our humankind, but by a sure surmise of the soul we see its very beckoning in Jesus Christ. The Beatitudes are not pious counsel, but axioms. Perhaps we should add that every man knows them to be such, until he begins to tamper with them in a proud intellect that demands "proof," or in a selfish will that breeds rebellion. Is there not a story of a child who read the Sermon on the Mount for the first time and rushed to her mother, crying, "Look what I've found! It's what I've known all along. Now we can live like this"? [21] By what other love can life cohere? The man who loves only himself is dungeoned, and the chill of the dungeon shows in his face. The man who loves only some neighbor is doomed to disappointment, for every human being fails in truth and at last dies. But the man who loves God made known in Christ, and thus loves his neighbor, has a sun in his sky around which his world revolves, and has light besides for every human loyalty and every earthly task. This involves an act of faith? Yes, but so does every human endeavor, not least our "objectivity." Faith gives life its courage and zest. "Thou shalt love the Lord thy God . . . and . . . thy neighbour as thyself."

V

The Commandment is more than basic faith for education. It guides educational process. "With all thy heart, and with all thy soul, and with all thy strength, and with all thy mind": there is cosmic thunder in that word "all." We ask how our distracted self can find unity. The Commandment is no full answer, but it is the highroad to the answer. The civil war within modern man is now openly admitted. Walter Lippmann has written of him that he is "one man today and another tomorrow, one person here and another there." [22] But that is cautious understatement, for modern man is fifty men in any place at any hour. In him there is a cattleyard, a fashion show, a bank teller's cage, a flower garden, and a monk's cell; and he cannot decide in which of them to live. He is one man on Sunday and another on Monday. He is one man in his mind and another in his feelings, for his mind (having stretched science beyond its ordained limits to make it criterion of the world) regards Durham Cathedral as structural stone according to blueprint, while his feelings see it as a shrine set above the winding river of man's years. He is one man in his heart and another in his strength of will, for he does what he secretly hates. Our slogans reveal the chasms in the modern self. "Don't mix business and pleasure." But why not? Should they not be mixed? That chasm has made business a treadmill and pleasure an escape. "Don't mix religion and politics." But, again, why not? That chasm has made religion a false or unreal piety and politics a morass.

Education shows its own variant of the current distraction. Functional psychology is no longer fashionable, but it still serves as reminder that all the forces of personality should find harmonious fulfillment, and that they cannot find it until they are obedient to some central loyalty. Even the most passive psychiatry, refusing to give the patient any counsel, posing as a cosmic ear, has some higher loyalty vaguely in view—to be called, perhaps, the self-reliant man. Psychiatry does not yet see that our brief dust posing as self-reliant is a pathetic comedy, or that a planet filled with self-reliant people would be something of a nightmare; but it does dimly realize, because it must, that the self must be harmonized around some hope or goal. "Thou shalt love the Lord thy God": is that the proper commitment? Education has stressed the mind, a fact with which we cannot quarrel, for the mind is education's central province. But education has forgotten the self's need of proportion. Has the result been intellectual conceit and the blindness that always waits on pride?

As for the conceit, it is such that every conviction must now give some academic password or be shot on sight. The man who loves his mother is promptly suspected of "mother fixation." The man who prays is pitied for overexcitement of the sex glands. Jesus Himself is dismissed because He did not live in a machine age or because apparently he does not satisfy our ever-changing doctrines of evolution. A preacher daily encounters the pettiness which challenges Christian faith to "prove it to me." "Prove" means proof by scientific tests, which are sensate and fractional; or proof by logic, which itself rests on axioms. Analysis that applies to potatoes does not apply to people, and formulas that gird a syllogism cannot describe a Bach chorale; and in any event a God who could be proved would not be God, but only a tin-pot god within the little measure of man's mind. Yet the average student is so steeped in the scientific fallacy that he cannot understand when the preacher says: "God has proved you, or you would not by trying to prove Him." The heart has its own reasons. So has any brave venture of the will. A faith that could be utterly proved by massed guns of argument that reduced all doubt to dust would not be faith but only coercion—much as a complete demonstration that "honesty is the best policy" would reduce all honesty to prudential shrewdness.

Thou canst not prove the Nameless, O my son,

. . . .

Thou canst not prove that thou art body alone,
Nor canst thou prove that thou art spirit alone,
Nor canst thou prove that thou art both in one.

. . . .

Thou canst not prove that I, who speak with thee,
Am not thyself in converse with thyself,
For nothing worthy proving can be proven,
Nor yet disproven. Wherefore thou be wise,
Cleave ever to the sunnier side of doubt,
And cling to Faith beyond the forms of Faith!

. . . .

She finds the fountain where they wailed "Mirage!" [23]

But in our time such lines seem "wishful thinking," so in bondage are we to the idolatry of scientism.

If the barrenness of intellectual pride is one result of education's overemphasis on mind, another result is emotional insecurity. Students emerge from college surfeited in mind but starved in feeling, each professor requiring so vast an amount of reading that, if it were ever done, it would become forcible feeding. The heart, denied its proper love (since greediness for facts can never be a kindling affair), feeds in weak students on petting parties and a steady diet of movies. The will, denied its venture of faith, becomes flabby, so that students are more and more uncertain of vocation. The soul, denied its proper worship, makes an idol of some football hero or (as in Germany) some quack political messiah. Thus academic life leads to repressions, and repressions invite septicemia. There would be as little hope in *unrelated* expression. The doctrine of self-expression might make sense if each energy within us lived in its own cage and could take an airing in its turn. But the sex instinct if given free rein rends the maternal instinct, and the fighting instinct if let loose destroys the home-making instinct, and the mind if overstressed breeds a fear of the emotions. Let us change the simile, for a circus in which the animals have broken loose in bedlam of bloodshed is a picture too cruelly true of our time. Let us choose a gentler simile: the instrumentalities of the self are in discord, like the tuning-up period before a symphony concert, until all are obedient to music and a leader.

So once more we are back home. Education is fractured unless it is held in a sovereign faith: "Thou shalt love the Lord thy God . . . and . . . thy neighbour as thyself." The four great words of Lear's shining speech perhaps correspond with the four compass words of the Commandment. Said Lear to the commoner in their prison: "So we'll live," that being the all-embracing word; "and pray," that being the satisfaction of the *soul;* "and sing," that being the expression of the *heart;* "and tell old tales," that being the food of the *mind,* since education is the discovery and interpretation of the stories God has written on earth and sky and man's nature; "and laugh," that being grace of friendship and *strength* of faith. By such means men do live:

So we'll live,
And pray, and sing, and tell old tales, and laugh
At gilded butterflies, and hear poor rogues
Talk of court news; and we'll talk with them too,
Who loses and who wins; who's in, who's out;
And take upon 's the mystery of things,
As if we were God's spies: and we'll wear out,
In a wall'd prison, packs and sets of great ones
That ebb and flow by the moon.[24]

The secularist says that the man of religious faith is suffering from "repressions." But why not turn the tables? The religionist has as much right to turn them as the secularist to set them. Why not say that the secularist is a man suffering from the repression of his innate faith? There is evidence!

VI

These strictures from a churchman are made under sense of sin, for if the school has laid too much stress on mind, some religion has been an orgy of emotion with too little place for mind and even less place for forthright exercise of will. Sense of sin is here joined with sense of inability, for if the challenge should come to this book, "Show how the college can correct the imbalance, and find a due proportion," this book can give no full answer. The answer must come from within education. The search is on, for one of the few heartening signs of our day is education's resolve to set its house in order. Such a book as Sir Walter Moberly's *The Crisis in the University*[25] is more than a portent: it could be the thrust of creative revolution. The Commandment itself provides a ground plan for a new order of schools, but educators and friends of education must draw the detailed blueprints.

A college can provide chance for a man's *strength* of venture and will. It can link itself with the need of the community. Medicine has internships. So has agriculture, on an actual farm; and social hygiene, in an actual community. Students take courses in race and culture. But why at a distance? In America that field is just outside the door, with chance to prove a friendship while conducting a study. One group of college men asked the local community council for the trees that had been cut down to widen a highroad, and the council agreed; whereupon the college used the trees for the benefit of Negroes living in neighboring shacks. That act was small? Yes, but it showed a main intention, and God takes such a will for the deed. The college textbook said: "Attack must be made on discrimination." Those college men made no attack, but at least they made a foray; and meanwhile they were learning, for we learn only from life. Can any problem be solved by the mind alone? The ancients knew that the problem of the hare and the tortoise is hardly soluble on paper; it is solved in life. Perhaps only so can any problem be solved. For life actually is not a problem to be solved by some slick formula, but living clay to be shaped by living men into worth and loveliness.

A college can provide opportunity for a man's *heart*. The curriculum time given to science is disproportionately large. This appraisal does not disparage science. Science has bestowed physical blessings through medicine, intellectual blessings through the gift of the printing machine, blessings of friendship through means of travel; and by its rigor of truth it has enriched religion, for such honor is implicit devotion. But scientific tests are still sensate and still analytical, and unless men can gather enough self-control and reverence to use the mammoth forces which science has released, science itself is under threat. Physical science is easier by far than the social sciences or the arts, not to mention the task of the church, or would be easier if it had not reached the boundary line where it becomes philosophy. To mend an automobile is relatively simple, if only because the automobile cannot "answer back"; but to mend the disordered mind or broken heart of the passengers is another matter. Thus we are masters of a bombing plane and novices in the statecraft of peace. Is it not time that we gave ourselves to the harder task? But we shall not do so if we lavish *undue* energy on science, or if we continue to describe the atomic bomb as "the greatest discovery of our generation." So omnipresent is the disproportionate influence of science that even the study of Shakespeare is in some quarters shallowed into semantics. Again there are signs of hope, for the scientists themselves are now in the vanguard of those who would lead us into a new citizenship. But do they realize that the humanities must be a much larger part of the preparation for that quest?

The college can give opening to a man's *soul*. How? Through worship. What other way than through worship—worship implicit or explicit, private and corporate? In some colleges and universities the chapel has disappeared; in others it never existed. In some it is mainly an assembly where college societies make announcements and cheerleaders give pep talks pending the next football game; in others worship is still held, but more in deference to tradition than in any vital fervor. The word "chapel" comes from the Latin *cappa*, a cloak. The cloak, given by St. Martin to a beggar, was preserved in a room called *cappella*:[26] thus chapel. St. Martin's philanthropy was not the focus of his life. His rigorous but tolerant mind, which opposed heresy yet withheld friendship from bishops who slew heretics, was not his central flame. These graces were the fruit of his life, not its root. The root was adoring prayer and praise. Chapel, the shrine of a St. Martin commitment to God, is the place where we now make announcements! Meanwhile there must be no "compulsory chapel." The word "compulsory" in that setting is a fascination. The dean insists that a man take a language during his first year, but nobody speaks bitterly of "compulsory language." The professor in fine arts requires a student to listen to certain music, but nobody complains rabidly about "compulsory music." But if someone says, "This college believes that you should expose yourself as student to the scriptures and praise that have overthrown old cruelties, richly colored our civilization, and nerved men to glad martyrdom," there is instant cry of "Tyranny!" Some universities have no central worship. They do not offer even a live option between the secular and sacred. The church-related college at least offers a live option, for there is no shortage of secularism on any campus. Then why would we not more accurately condemn the secular universities as "compulsory secularism"? Secularism leaves mankind with no hearthfire, no altar, no window "opening on . . . perilous seas" [27] or on the serenity of stars, and no defense (if doom would then matter) against the subliminal irrationalisms that erupt beneath a Godless society to destroy it.

"Heart," "mind," "soul," and "strength" in Bible language are not rigidly distinct words. The Bible never lent encouragement to functional psychology: any reader can see for himself that it anticipates our "depth" psychology. In the Hebrew the word "heart" has some of the force of our word "will," while the Hebrew word for "soul" is not alien from our word "life." Thus the four words, while each has its own thrust, still merge—in a commitment to God. The scientist Faraday, when he was a boy selling newspapers, put head and arms through the iron railing of a gate. He was philosopher as well as scientist, for he asked himself: "If my head is on one side of the gate, and my heart and body on the other, on which side am I?" Some versions of the story hold that just then someone suddenly opened the gate, Faraday being almost decapitated, and that he exclaimed in the rueful memory of later life, "The whole of a man should be on one side of the gate." [28] The gate is opening in our time because crisis, while it is always judgment, as the original meaning of the word clearly shows, is also a summons and an opening. Church and school alike had better be all on one side of the gate—heart, mind, soul, and strength.

VII

What would happen to a college or university if such a ground plan were adopted? While graduate schools would still have rightful place, the curriculum of the average college would be sharply pruned. No school can offer every course under heaven, for the good reason that no mind or group of minds can comprehend, much less marshal and interpret, the bewildering array of discovered facts. Every school must "pick and choose" in deliberate self-limitation. Such restriction is distressful to our mortal pride, but unfortunately there is no escape, for these limits to learning are the very stuff of our mortality. But why should a college wish or try to teach everything? Knowledge is a more precious treasure than information, and wisdom is more to be desired than knowledge. A cafeteria offering every known food either would starve a man as he wandered down long aisles of food unable to decide which to choose, or it would ruin his digestion in his attempt to sample every dish. That description is not altogether inapplicable to some state universities, but its purpose here is to underscore the perhaps painful fact that in the brief span of life a man must choose, and that he had better choose staple and life-giving foods. In other words, education also must accept the bounds of finiteness. A school that denies itself the specializations which graduate colleges may properly indulge has its compensation–namely, the chance to gather knowledge into a creative synthesis, in lack of which education in our time spreads like a marsh instead of flowing like a river. For in the case of any man or college some books, however worthy, must go unread; and some endeavors, however beckoning, must be renounced. For brief life is man's portion, and the good can be the enemy of the best. That is why all life is under the Commandment: "Thou shalt love the Lord thy God . . . and . . . thy neighbour as thyself."

The necessary limitation in curriculum might be an added boon in this regard: the decision on what to omit and what to include would require criteria and might thus carry the college to a now sadly lacking unity of purpose. Then perhaps there might be a better diet than "fact":

> That frost of fact by which our wisdom gives
> Correctly stated death to all that lives.[29]

The student then might find a main objective. Lord Morley perhaps disavowed faith or left it unnurtured, but he recognized that faith can integrate the self; for he wrote of Gladstone that "all his endeavors were in his own mind one," [30] meaning one in the love of God. Life for Gladstone was not a widespread swamp: a channel had been cut out for him, and the river flowed strongly and singingly to the sea. Thus the necessity of limitation, whether in a man's work or in a college curriculum, is itself a summons to think through the meaning of life. What *is* education? It is far more than an intellectual exercise. It should lead men out to their destiny. There are those who believe that man's destiny is defined re-deemingly in Christ. Perhaps the tragedy of our times, far from disproving the claim, has disproved its denial.

The Commandment stands. It is no mere plea or per-suasion: it stands "from the foundation of the world." [31] Neither school nor church can break it: in the attempt they break only themselves. In our era faith has been in eclipse. The twentieth century has thus far been a crippled century, a deformed child of a man-centeredness that has settled on our world, the only century that has tried to live without an avowed faith. But when faith is not avowed, it is not escaped; for always men must cleave to some faith. The hidden faith of the early twentieth century has been the cult of success in practical affairs and an arid scientism in matters of the mind. The success never dreamed it could be failure, and the scientism never suspected that it was largely the reflection of a divergent culture. But now we are driven to reask the primal question: What is the true faith? We may be sure, since we are creatures, that the true faith will not be merely or primarily our choice; for it will first choose us, through the axioms of our human nature.

The present darkness may not soon pass. Propaganda, the deliberate perversion of words and meanings for the sake of selfishness in trade and politics, has made us strangers to truth; and the resort to force has not only filled our world with bitterness and confusion, but made us dubious concerning any better kind of power. Meanwhile scientism hints that mind may be only chemistry. If thought is mere phosphorescence playing about a pulp of brain, it is foolish to speak of truth and falsehood, for then all thought (including scientific thought) is a wandering fire soon lost in night. If conscience is only a poor relativism of changing custom, it is foolish to speak of right and wrong, for then there is neither landmark nor law. From this nothingness wise men will draw back as from a black precipice. Church and school must unite to reavow a new-old faith: "Thou shalt love the Lord thy God . . . and . . . thy neighbour as thyself." Then men may cease to walk toward judgment in the cold and gloom of their own shadow: they can turn and face the Light.

Chapter Two . COMMUNITY

SOME YEARS AGO there was a popular song, not more maudlin than its fellows, that concluded with the resolve to "let the rest of the world go by." [1] It would be unfair to say that education has taken that vow. But certainly it has lived of late in that disregard. The phrase "town and gown" shows the cleavage. At worst the "town" has scorned the "highfalutin" ideas of the learned, and the "gown" has disdained the "ignorant masses," while even at best neither has confessed a shining commonalty. The endowments and tuition fees of our colleges have come in large measure from hard toil: the scholar is carried on the backs of laborers. Of course there has been a return gift: wisdom distills into the everyday world from the teacher. Our material wealth, the livelihood on which all endeavors rest, comes from land, labor, and the idea. Hand and mind are thus always linked to develop the freely given resources of nature. It is tragic that the bond between hand and mind should be broken; for then manual toil becomes blind, and mental toil becomes merely abstract—drawn away from reality. The myth of Antaeus[2] tells that he was invincible so long as he had even one toe on the common earth, but that any puny foe could conquer him when he was up in the air. Perhaps our education, and therefore our whole society, has suffered from that severance. The Commandment bids us love "thy neighbour as thyself." Jesus declared that the second part is "like" the first. The word means *almost the same as* or *is implied*. If the Commandment is valid, that second part also is a yoke on education.

I

But *is* that "like" commandment valid? All pious sentiment aside, is it possible to hold our neighbor's life in equal concern with our own, to say nothing of keeping both within a steadfast love for God? There are over two hundred deaths a day in New York City. Who could carry that daily weight of sympathy in sorrow? There were in one particular year over four hundred births each day in the same city, and most of them spelled joy. Who could even apprehend that vast gladness? Narrow the demand: can I love my neighbor as myself on a crowded subway train? In truth a rhetorical question! There is a story of a wedged-in passenger mildly protesting, "Excuse me, madam, but that's my nose you're blowing." So let us bring the demand within still smaller limits: can any scholar love the people on near-by Main Street? God will not forsake us for asking honest questions. Besides, we shall hereinafter face the fact of failure and ask what to do—or rather what God has done.

E. W. Howe, a famous editor living at the turn of our century, was doubly honest, for he wrote: "I do not love my neighbor as myself, and apologize to no one. I treat my neighbor as fairly and politely as I hope to be treated, but there is no law in common sense or nature ordering me to go beyond that." [3] But he was wrong. There may be no law in what we call common sense, but there is a law in human nature and a deeper law in God. If a family on the other side of the tracks has smallpox, we must treat them with as much care as if they were blood brothers, if only because the smallpox may cross the tracks to invade the campus. We must treat in like concern a poverty-stricken nation on the other side of the world, if only because they may embrace communism and then threaten our life. For all men *are* blood brothers. Life allows no man to live isolated in an ivory tower: food and clothing have to come from surrounding factories and fields.

So there *is* a law: "Thou shalt love thy neighbour as thyself." It begs no man's pardon. E. W. Howe admitted the law while trying to deny it, for the phrase "as fairly and politely as I hope to be treated" itself traces an ultimate requirement. No warning Voice thunders from the sky, except perhaps in an atomic bomb; but as for the Commandment in New York City, a tugboat strike recently left college classrooms under threat of cold. The campus had not realized until then that it depended on grimy men who bring coal by tugboat across the Hudson River. But *can* we keep the Commandment? Not in our little human "love." The word is *agape,* not *philia;*[4] "love" in the Commandment is God's gift, and only so can it be man's response. No man is asked to play the role of Atlas, much less to try to do what only God can do. But we are asked to let God's love have place in us through prayer and worship: "And be ye kind," therefore, "tender-hearted, forgiving one another," in love, "even as God for Christ's sake hath forgiven you."[5] The Commandment is not canceled in any college or church.

Neighborhood cannot be narrowed. The question "Who is my neighbour?" was addressed to Jesus in a day when the Jew regarded only fellow Jews as neighbors, and when he was sure that some of them were beyond the pale. Jesus did not require the questioner to enter into every man's joy and sorrow, for that is not possible: the heart would break under the strain. But Jesus did tell the story of the good Samaritan,[6] a man of a despised race. In America the story might have been about the good Negro. "Who is my neighbour?" He was only "a certain man." No name was given, no detail of age or caste, no mention of college degree, no account of virtue or delinquency. Only two facts were told: the man was a man, and he was in need. So a neighbor is anyone in need whom we see as we journey. Radar has enabled us to see a long way. It will not avail us to say that "we have nothing in common." Perhaps only a scientific civilization could have coined a phrase so untrue. We have humanity in common, and therefore we have tears and laughter in common, and failure and the need of pardon. As compared with this oneness, how deep does education go? We make our entrance into life through one miracle of birth and our exit through one valley of the shadow, and in between that "coming in" and that "going out" we are one little caravan bound on one pilgrimage. Education cannot stand above or beyond that pilgrimage, however it may try. It ought not to try.

II

Before we explore further the momentous import of community for education, proper sequence perhaps calls us to come to terms with two strange words in the Commandment: "thy neighbour *as thyself*." In their full grammar they seem to contradict the rest of the royal law: "Thou shalt love thyself." Maybe that is why the two words in their Commandment setting have been so largely ignored. We say in mild disgust of some self-centered man: "He certainly loves himself." More certainly Jesus could never have commended that kind of self-love. Then what kind? Some measure of self-concern no man can escape. Even a saint must spend some time in eating and sleeping. That is to say, he must cater to his own elemental hungers; and even though he may leap from bed vowing to dedicate the new day to God, he must soon feed his own mouth. Though individualism has been almost disastrous in our Western world, a complete communism is not possible; for the paper on which a communist writes his creed for *Tass* or *Pravda* must be his individual possession, at least while he uses it. Each man inhabits a body, his own share of space-time. So "common property" is always something of a misnomer. A man's hand or mind is more intimately his own than a pen, and can be shared only in part. But all this is far from the selfishness of "Joe loves Joe," and much farther from the Commandment.

Yet "thy neighbour as thyself" does not involve us in contradiction, or if it does, the contradiction carries us back into a Presence. Here is the apparent contradiction: "Self-preservation is the first law of life," but "he that loseth his life . . . shall find it." [7] Another expression of the riddle is this: J. C. and A. W. Hare say that "the first step to self-knowledge is self-distrust," [8] but Emerson says, "Trust thyself: every heart vibrates to that iron string." [9] Each dictum strikes us as true, so the contradiction must be below the surface. In point of fact *the contradiction is in human nature itself*, about which education has entertained such a naïve optimism. "Self-distrust" means misgiving about a transitory and evilly biased self, and "trust thyself" means the alignment of prayer and will with the strangely transcendent self which enables a man to say of his lower life: "I was wrong," or, "I shall soon die." Can any man look at Buchenwald and deny the evil bias in human nature under the enticements of demonism? So education is now confronted by a deeper challenge: How shall it deal with the cleft in human nature, and which self shall it serve? On what power shall it call if it would expel the demon and set free the saint?

But let us follow through our inquiry into a true self-love. Plainly Jesus meant that a man is to choose his higher self against his lower self. His higher self is, by every presumption in the teaching of Jesus, linked with God; and his neighbor's higher self is likewise linked with God. That is why the *first* commandment is that we love God, and why the "second" is both pendant from and "like" the first; for only as a man loves God can he truly love his neighbor as himself, and only then is love of his neighbor and love of himself one indivisible love. To cite a negative instance, "honor among thieves" is honor only on the level of a transitory and perverted self, because it does not first love God. To cite a positive instance, no one could wisely wish that Bach had deserted his music to run a soup kitchen. He loved God (why do we forget the text of scripture set at the head of the chorale?), and therefore he loved his higher self in God's gift of music, and therefore he deeply loved his neighbor. That instance is too true for mere mention. Bach [10] did sometimes run a charity society, for he had twenty children and was buried in a pauper's grave. The necessity of bread and butter was perhaps his Antaeus contact with the earth and doubtless gave realism to his music. But music was his very self, in such intensity that when he was given four weeks' leave of absence from his church organ to study with Buxtehude, he stayed four months and had to be ordered home and reprimanded. Surely God liked Bach A.W.O.L. better than He liked the reprimand. For music was still Bach's higher self, and Bach loved himself in God and therefore loved his neighbor as himself.

Thus both an insidious individualism and a slapdash altruism are outside the Commandment. As for the individualism, we shall see that *that* has been largely the presupposition of an education pretending to have no presuppositions. As for the slapdash altruism, "service to mankind" calls for more than a pleasant smile and a good intention. It calls for more than a resolve to "give myself for the sake of the world," for that resolve ignores the questions, What kind of self? and, What kind of world? Besides, we know people of whom we should hope that they will not give themselves to the world, or that the world will reject the gift. Altruism calls for more than what John Dewey has termed "the definite substitution of a social purpose, controlling methods of teaching and discipline and materials of study, for the traditional individualistic aim." [11] Our sympathies are enlisted by the proposal, but we must ask: What social purpose, judged by what criterion? The quoted phrase is typical Deweyism. He dismisses with his right hand all godly assumptions in the name of early twentieth-century science, and then calls them back with his left hand but with due care to hide their return under high-sounding generalities. Fortunately this bluff is now being called. Education always has, and must have, some presuppositions. This book pleads that *the* presupposition is the Great Commandment, because by judgment and mercy that is the axiom to which men return. When Lincoln told the Committee of Seventy from Missouri that he wished to conduct his administration so that, even though he lost all other friends, "I shall at least have one friend left, and that friend shall be deep down inside me," [12] he was actually appealing to the axiom of the Commandment: "Thou shalt love the Lord thy God . . . and . . . thy neighbour as thyself."

III

Education is the ward, if not the child, of the prevailing culture. It owes a debt to its home, both in gratitude for good received and in resolve to improve upon its upbringing. How long will educators pretend that they obey only "reason," and that reason is the impartial arbiter of the human scene? Reason also is shaped and colored by contemporary attitudes. How long will fact-finders pose as deliverers? The man who proposes that our "main need is to get at the facts" is a blind and cruel leader, whatever his good intention; for he might as well be saying, "We shall have a home as soon as we find a lumberyard." Psychology has shown us that reason is colored by rationalizing, stained by the reasoner's desire and will. The more strange therefore that psychology itself should sometimes claim scientific realism,[13] and doubly strange that education, paying a due and deserved respect to psychology's stress on the danger of rationalizing, should find in its own processes only a "strictly objective mind"! Facts so-called are gathered according to some principle or purpose. The differences between schools of psychology or of sociology are not primarily differences of fact, for they have roughly the same facts, but of interpretation; and the interpretation in each instance rests on some covert faith or unfaith—on the doctrine of human nature, for instance, implied in the phrase "our main need is the facts"! The proposal that "we cannot get at truth except by objective study" has reached the pitch of comedy, as if it would say to Albert Schweitzer, "You cannot understand Bach because you are musically and emotionally prejudiced in his favor." When a man trained only in science asks me, a preacher, if I think I can give an unbiased account of Christian faith, perhaps I should reply in friendship, "Yes, if you think you can."

But is not theological thinking similarly "slanted"? Yes, of course. This coloration from the community is inevitable and not all misfortune. The Protestant Reformation coincided, by no accident, with the ferment of nationalism and the revolt against the narrow limits of scholastic philosophy. Had Luther been born fifty years earlier, he might have met the fate of Jan Huss. Liberal theology of the last generation was influenced by boom years in industry. Neo-orthodoxy in our time has a "tragic sense of life" [14] because it lives in the shadow of world tragedy. Protestant denominationalism, as likewise certain traits in current Romanism and Judaism, was prompted in part by a prevailing individualism. We should neither evade these facts nor shrink from the issues which they raise. *Is there in man a mind above, as well as within, the dominant culture? Is this transcendent quality of mind met and blessed by Transcendence? It is hard to see how otherwise man himself can be better than bias.* Such a book as Richard Niebuhr's *Christ and Culture*[15] has implications for educators as well as churchmen.

For education, not least in its scientific outlook, is also affected by the mores. The "little red schoolhouse" was designed to meet the needs of a pioneer society. Our cult of academic degrees is not alien from a world that has exalted individual "success." Our greed for facts is not utterly divorced from the prevailing greed for goods. The itch for "strict objectivity," as though a man could leap out of mortal limitation to view the cosmos with angel eyes, is in measure due to our recent overweening self-confidence. The naïve idea that science is a new messiah is not unlinked with the current man-centeredness. The mushrooming of technologies in the educational curriculum reflects our era's trust in gadgets, the half-belief that radio and radar can somehow save the world. The clutter of departments in a modern university, no two departments easily speaking the same language, parallels the distraction and dismemberment of the modern world. The secularism of education, so earthy that it even tries to reduce concepts to chromosomes, may be not so much a considered judgment as the stain of a society that in practice has tried to ignore God.

Thus reason is not neutral, whatever be the educational claim, but filled with hidden assumptions. To cite one among many, it has a ludicrously untrue doctrine of human nature: it assumes that man is a reasonable creature who, when given enough facts, will promptly order his world in reasonableness. So entrenched is this assumption, offered in the name of "impartial science," that perhaps only an atomic bomb can dislodge it. Hitler and Stalin, rightly observing that education is covertly colored by a false culture, have wrongly proposed that it shall be overtly controlled by *their* culture. That is the issue in our time, and scientism must bear no small share of blame![16] No culture should control education, at least until culture can be equated with the kingdom of God. The cruel totalitarianisms of our time have not yet attained that sanctity! But education cannot escape the mores, and therefore education is under more urgent summons to give both critique and guidance to its encompassing culture. John Dewey's plea that we substitute "a social purpose . . . for the traditional individualistic aim" [17] is in measure valid, or would be if he proposed proper tests of social purpose. His further plea, "I would urge teachers to ally themselves with organized labor," [18] raises more doubts. That could spell subservience to a proletarian culture. If that link were forged, it would soon have to be broken, for mass power is as vulnerable to the corruption which waits on human pride as is class power. What *is* the test for men and society? Since reason is not neutral but makes assumptions (as witness the covert and false assumptions of our scientism), what is the *true* assumption? In one assumption mankind, we may or must surmise, was born. To that assumption mankind again and again returns. Obedience to it has found a secret joy. The flouting of it has found always such desolation as our rebellious age now knows. "Thou shalt love the Lord thy God . . . and . . . thy neighbour as thyself." The gift of that love, its interpretation and cutting edge and radiant content, is seen in Jesus. Education, being blessed and yet disfigured by community, must repay the blessing and take no revenge for the disfigurement.

IV

Then how can a college keep the bonds of community? Perhaps this book has no right to try to answer that question. Teachers are in most instances valuable citizens, finer by far than the implicit creed in which their curricula and profession are held. They live by faith, not by the dull factualism which they may be asked to teach. In many an instance their devotion puts other callings to shame. A teacher pours out mind and heart for forty years, and dies poor as he has lived poor, though rich in the gratitude of successive generations of children; and meanwhile we allow a fortune to some man who has only the mercenary shrewdness to "play the market" or the inventiveness to make a new gadget or a tricky advertising device. It is doubtful that any society can endure cut and crippled by such inequality. The reorientation in education must come from within, and teachers themselves are more and more aware of an impasse in their calling. They are making creative changes,[19] as witness the new place being offered to religion not only in privately supported schools, but also in state universities. It seems only ingratitude and temerity that this little book should suggest how education can fulfill the demands of community.

Yet plainly a college should keep unblocked the channels of neighborliness with its immediate and wider community. Perhaps the tension between town and gown cannot be wholly removed, for men in their finitude and failure easily become strangers, but this tension can be relieved. If the town's contempt for "larnin'" is a psychological defense, the gown's aloofness may savor of intellectual conceit. The down-to-earth wisdom of the common man is perhaps the core of all human wisdom. The college needs the community even in the intellectual sphere; the community needs the college—as witness the new methods in agriculture. There should thus be a mutual learning between gown and town in resolute friendship. My friend the farmer who said of his preacher, "He's like summer lightning: fills the sky and hits nowhere," can teach me, a teacher of homiletics; and my friend the nurseryman who said of the hillside patch of second-growth Michigan scrub, of which someone had spoken disparagingly, "It holds the world together," does not lack profundity. Meanwhile both the farmer and the nurseryman owe much to the state university, not alone or mainly in practical ways, but through steady percolation of truth. Thus friendship between gown and town spells mutual gifts. A group of youngsters from the tenements in my parish, when they were asked if they would receive a "Christian delegation" from a famous university, replied through one of their number: "Yes, if they make it a round table: I've learned something from a milk route in the West Forties." Some of the endowment money of colleges has come from the faces of the poor. The land grants of Texas schools are by direct grace of the pioneers. So education should live in neighborliness. That warmth *is* found on many a campus, and it is a cheerful fire.

The college should not become a welfare society, though it must fulfill its share in that compassion. The college should not become a church, though the church is in sore need of the lay leadership that the schools can give. The community service of a college is not mainly in these fields or even in interchange of students across national lines, though our times cryingly require that wisdom. The college should not become a crusade against racial prejudice, though that witness in a college is demanded both by our shame and our peace. The college should rather render in the community its characteristic service. Bach's best sharing was through his own gift In England the adult education movement has been seminal, not only in spread of knowledge, but in a true unity in the nation. It has helped to bridge chasms, not alone between labor and education, but between government and labor, and between education and the church. The bridge may seem as yet only a rope flung across the gulf; but even if it were no more, a rope is the first item in building a strong span. Teachers in the movement readily agree that they have found within it apt and eager pupils who, by wisdom drawn from daily life, have reversed the parts to become teachers to the teacher. Perhaps schools and colleges have a better chance than churches to become centers of good citizenship and of neighborhood. Labor might thus become informed, instead of merely embattled; and group privilege might thus be enlightened, instead of merely entrenched. Best of all, a new friendship might redeem the estranged blocs of our modern society.

There is another community service which only a college can render—the unashamed avowal of its convictions against the tyrannies and demagogueries that so easily beset us. In some areas a college may and must maintain its attitude of suspended judgment, as, for example, concerning a cure for leukemia or the extent of the universe. But how can any college suspend judgment on such a portent as Hitler and the conditions that invited him? A German pastor said in conviction of sin: "I should have spoken, and did not speak." [20] That remorse is inescapable for a college also unless it bears its witness. The arid intellectualism of German universities helped to create the vacuum of nonbelief into which Hitlerism rushed, since human nature also abhors a vacuum. Community and student body alike have suffered too long from professors to whom all things are merely relative or academic. Students are beginning to say of such "teaching" what a keen-minded girl said of her psychoanalyst: "He wouldn't tell me anything, even if I stood on my head on his desk." Who knows, perhaps he had nothing to tell. Admittedly the line between impartial judgment on the one hand and conviction on the other is hard to draw. But can the literature professor teach these lines without comment?

> One mite wrung from the labourer's hands
> Shall buy and sell the miser's lands;
> Or, if protected from on high,
> Does that whole nation sell and buy.[21]

Such lines are not semantics to be studied in merely scientific mind; still less the succeeding lines:

> He who mocks the infant's faith
> Shall be mocked in age and death.
>
> . . . .
>
> If the Sun and Moon should doubt
> They'd immediately go out.[22]

Or, to cite another instance, economics now knows that labor is not to be regarded primarily as a commodity. An economist does not need to swallow whole all of John Maynard Keynes to be aware that the "law" of supply and demand has now an insufficient or subordinate authority. Even conservative economists know in our time that new criteria, however vaguely they may loom up through the fog, must now be honored–zest in toil, security, friendship. Then should not the economist say so for the public good? Not least for labor's good, since labor in its turn bids fair (or foul) to surrender to the economic fallacy of treating man as economic man, and to stress wages and hours instead of the creativeness and friendliness of toil.

Loyalty oaths have sharpened the contention that a college must speak its convictions. There was a day in our American life when a man was deemed innocent until proved guilty, but now he is guilty unless he proves himself innocent. The difference is not great perhaps; but, then, neither is a camel's nose in the tent. The trouble is that a camel follows its nose. Did not Hitler use the device of loyalty oaths? A justifiable sternness toward communists does not require us to coddle fascists. Will someone say that this area of conviction is not the task of education? That is what German professors said. The issue admittedly raises again the question, What *is* education? Whatever it is, it will be conducted in some faith, if only in the covert faith of scientism—that man is a creature to be fed on facts. Why not in a worthy faith? One faith has stood the test: "Thou shalt love the Lord thy God . . . and . . . thy neighbour as thyself."

V

Perhaps education's best contribution to the life of the community is the creation of a true community within the school itself. The fine original meaning of college, *collegium*, easily slips from memory. Perhaps universities with a vast enrollment cannot fulfill the word. Any group grown too large, whether school or church or business, may be in danger of neglecting the person, and thus of ultimate collapse. Evolutionists avow that no giant breeds a giant. The largest animal known, the Antarctic whale, has its ears blocked, and its eyes blinded—by a huge upturned lip! The cult of bigness raises issues which our age must explore. Whatever the answer, teachers and pupils should be colleagues: a *collegium*. Oxford and Cambridge set the pattern. Sir Walter Moberly's *The Crisis in the University* comes from that setting, and pleads in sorrow that the pattern has been discarded. Of course the original bond of the *collegium*, both in England and in America, was Christian faith. Howard Lowry in his book *The Mind's Adventure* has strikingly reminded us of this fact.[23] But now? Fraternities and sororities, far from providing a substitute for the *col-*

legium, are perhaps likelier to bring new distractions. The college tends to become a degree mill rather than a comradeship.

For mark what has happened. The man voracious for facts, as the mouth is greedy for food or the hand for money, is now honored—he, not the man who in lowliness seeks wisdom. The man who outstrips others in learning receives rewards—he, not the man who falls back to help others in the race. The man who plays the lone hand and pores over books till late hours wins plaudits—he, not the man so compassionately aware of the sins and sorrows of the race that he cannot live content in academic seclusion. Perhaps these prize winners are all budding Bachs, cultivating their gift in reluctant sanctuary that hereafter it may be dedicated to God and man; but the suspicion will not down that many of them seek the academic equivalent for what our raucous age calls "success." In our technical schools, with courses in business management and advertising, careerism is almost avowed; and any incipient St. Francis finds himself in an alien realm. Perhaps a college in these regards is only the reflection of an acquisitive society, the microcosm of a clamant and selfish world.

But suppose the college were more truly a *collegium*, what would become of educational standards? Again we are obliged to inquire for a sound definition of education. But perhaps even "book-learning" standards would be better honored. For a man cannot study except in some home of the spirit: he must have some security as a person. Even an Antarctic expedition has a ship as base, some "Little America" in the wilderness. Can there ever be adequate personal security in a college dedicated to facts and suspended judgment? If the college were more truly a comradeship, would not scholarship thereby be enhanced? At present 50 per cent of our sicknesses have an accompaniment or origin of emotional maladjustment, and there is little evidence that education has stemmed the flood. A cursory glance would seem to show that education may rather be increasing the flood by an overdemand on the brain. It is not good for a mind to be alone, and it is not good for a man to be alone. A *collegium* would correct that imbalance and so actually aid study. In any event there may be more important standards than educational standards, even for education; for education is still only an adjective to the noun life. Education also is under the Commandment. A school cannot endure as a concourse of strangers greedy for facts, or as an academic reflection of a lonely competitive world. Its best gift to the community is itself to become a radiant community in mind and spirit.

VI

I have hardly mentioned the remoteness of curriculum from current life. But there is a wide gap, and plainly the closing of that gap is a debt which education owes both to the student and to the community. History taught only as a list of dates, battles, and kings to be committed to unwilling memory is fortunately done or dying; for the path opened by John Richard Green,[24] by which history is seen as social movement as well as "historical event," is now a well-trodden road. But there is still an impossible striving after "objective history," since even historians have taken to wearing scientism's blinders; and in many socially aware histories the social movements have ceased to move. Even the resurgence that brought the Magna Charta has become a painted ship on a painted river rather than a traffic on that living stream on which our lives are carried. Wallace B. Donham reports one college graduate as remarking that "he had concentrated in history in college but that not once could he remember having any aspect of history discussed in terms of its bearing on his life or on current problems." [25]

Perhaps other subjects have been even more remote. Even economics has tended to become an intellectual game played with counters and symbols. A. N. Whitehead has written:

> Instead of this single unity, we offer children Algebra, from which nothing follows; Geometry, from which nothing follows; Science, from which nothing follows; History,

from which nothing follows; a couple of languages, never mastered; and lastly, most dreary of all, Literature, represented by plays of Shakespeare, with philological notes and short analyses of plot and character to be in substance committed to memory. Can such a list be said to represent Life, as it is known in the midst of the living of it?[26]

Probably these strictures are too severe, for who among us cannot gratefully remember teachers who made their lectures live? But that there is real truth in the protest is sufficiently shown by the fact that most college graduates are glad on commencement day to forget what they have learned. They shuffle off the academic unrealism because they must now confront life.

This remoteness of curriculum is the more hurtful in a time of swift social change. Through the undue liberty of the elective system students have become, not trained minds, but wanderers through a bargain basement where men

> talk of many things:
> Of shoes—and ships—and sealing-wax—
> Of cabbages—and kings—
> And why the sea is boiling hot—
> And whether pigs have wings.[27]

The requirement that the student early choose a major study (to offset the danger of electives?) then locks him in a "department" with its own lingo and almost its own laws, where he has scant contact with other studies and even less with the outside world. Latterly the choice in majors has run to the sciences and technologies because schools have been in unwitting subservience to an industrial era. Thus graduates have become the more incapable of navigating the crosscurrents and uncertainties, not to mention the human foibles, of daily life.

The specialist is notoriously a poor leader of man, for he tries to apply his local tenets to the total life. A professional parson in a city-planning commission overrun by politics might provide the illustration. Have we seen that the scientist is under similar handicap? The fact of indeterminism is now regnant even in his own science, and has brought a pretty impasse: the scientist must now become metaphysician and theologian! But he still assumes determinism. He moves in realms where laws are not broken. He works with generalizations to which there are no exceptions, for if exceptions occur, he promptly widens the generalizations. Thus he drifts further and further away from the actuality and mystery of the event—the hiding place of indeterminism. If he is a *practical* scientist, he busies himself with materials of predictable "behavior." Iron, when treated according to "law," does not curse, or thumb its nose, or go on strike, or overspend its income, or indulge in the dubious dramatics of a Senate investigation. Work with iron or even with electricity is comparatively a cinch; the local school board or the United Nations is anything but a cinch. Thus dominantly scientific education or even the typical liberal-arts training is a poor equipment for the rough-and-tumble of life.

The problem of the machine is only one instance, but a crucial instance. We lavish vast sums of money to make machines and other vast sums to train men to use them, but hardly pause to ask what effect machinery will have on character. Perhaps the machine is a Procrustean bed.[28] Perhaps men too short for the machine are stretched to proper length, and perhaps men too long for it are cut short in size; and perhaps all men are thus made unnaturally uniform, and perhaps that uniformity is prelude to death. The machine demands implicit obedience, and thus robs men of a rightful freedom. The machine in its easy solution of a mechanical problem beguiles men into thinking that the machine can solve a human problem, as witness our near deification of gadgets. The machine conditions men to an automatic response, and thus prepares them for the lockstep demanded by a Hitler. The machine turns men's minds from men to materials, from life to lifelessness, from the social need to the tricky contrivance, and therefore ultimately from vocation to vacuity. We need machines, and they are a blessing. Yes, but we need them, like all other blessings, only in their time and place. What are their time and place? Our education hardly prepares us to give any kindling answer. The gulf between education and life must be bridged.

VII

"Who is sufficient for these things?" [29] Any thoughtful man, as he contemplates our tragic yet prophetic time, as he considers the demands now made on education or any other human endeavor, must exclaim over and over again, "Who is sufficient for these things?" Modern man, as he tries to cope with the forces now loose in his world, seems to be sent on a tiger hunt armed with only a peashooter. Have we not reached the end of merely human resource? Is history not doomed unless there is deliverance from beyond history? The requirement laid on us is ultimate, but our nature is only contingent; and so we are bereft unless the Ultimate lays hands on us. Therefore the Great Commandment: "Thou shalt love the Lord thy God." For love, especially *agape*, is a mutual word. A man can love God only because God has first loved him. Therein is the piercingness of New Testament vision: "We love . . . , because he first loved us." [30] The only sufficient faith for education, or business or politics, is one that will open life to a more-than-human power. The Commandment is a sovereignty and cannot be evaded, but in all its keywords it is also the plea and promise of Ultimate Love. This the church has proved, not by endless argument but by courageous faith. For, to cite an instance, when the church broke with the synagogue to dare all the uncertainties of the Gentile world under the dominance of the Roman empire, it trusted God and was not confounded. No politician would have endorsed that step as a "calculated risk," for by human tests it was an uncalculated foolhardiness. But it found wisdom and strength beyond itself. Loving God, it was loved of God.

Admittedly, to the Christian, Jesus Christ is the Commandment become incarnate, both in its challenge and in its assurance. If anyone should ask how we know, perchance that question is like asking how we know that the proportions of the Parthenon are right, or why an autumn woodland is a poignant loveliness. At long last truth is an immediacy. It cannot be proved by logic except as it first gives logic its only life. If God is God, we do not prove Him; for the attempt would be the blasphemy—the claim that we can hold Him in our mind, the setting up of ourselves as God. He is His own evidence. Christ, seriously pondered, strikes eternity into the mind. Presumably that is what Charles Lamb meant when he remarked that if Shakespeare entered the room, we would rise to greet him, but that if Christ came, we would kneel at His feet.[31] Yet so circumscribed is our vision by "scientific" tests, so forgetful are we that these tests themselves rest back on accepted axioms and a covert faith, that it is not enough for our generation to say that Jesus is His own proof. We counter with the proposal that Jesus may be a lay figure on which we have draped *our* ideals. But He is no lay figure. He is so sharp in challenge that constantly we try to evade Him. He is so troublesome that each generation hurries Him to some new Calvary, only to find that He is risen from the dead. In any event our ideals are not merely ours, for we are creatures; and far from our draping them on any figure, they are like wraiths moving in mist until someone comes to give them life. The fact is that Christ vivifies our ideals and also purifies them. No man lifted Him from His niche in history. No niche could hold Him. He comes, stronger than death, to lift us.

So the Commandment is no wordy abstraction: Christ etches it. The paradox of neighbor-love and self-love set in the higher paradox of human-love and God-love becomes life in Him:

> I love my neighbor as myself–
> Myself like him too, by his leave!
> Nor to his pleasure, power or pelf
> Came I to crouch, as I conceive![32]

How shall I love myself? As I love my neighbor. How shall I love him? As I love God. How shall I love God? As He has first loved the world through Jesus Christ. A Japanese friend brought an intricate box not easily opened. To force it open would only have broken it.

But there was a tiny hidden spring: it opened of itself when that was touched. Within there was a group of tiny globules, which when placed in water unfolded into everlasting flowers. That is a parable of man's heart. Faith in Christ, seemingly so frail, is the hidden spring. The box cannot be forced, as any cult of brute power must learn; and it is not empty, for its "natural longings" open into everlasting flowers.

In what other faith can a *collegium* be firmly held? Factualisms and suspended judgment cannot give coherence. The nature of the bond is the sharp issue in any society. A lynching mob is held by blood lust and unreasoning hatred, and therefore soon splinters into shamed and lonely men. A football crowd has excitement for its bond, plus some devotion to athletics and a not unworthy measure of group loyalty, but the bond is ephemeral: nobody could enjoy a football game for more than a few hours at a time. A symphony concert has music for its bond; and that is stronger, for if music is not God's word, it is at least the rustling of His robe. What can bind a *collegium?* Not truth as intellectually conceived. That faith would be too cold, and hides too many unexamined assumptions. But truth as a commandment, which is yet mutual love, with a Man to speak it in the incarnate Word—that is the bond.

We should not misunderstand: the bond would be no promise that all problems would vanish, still less that the school or college would win an instant eminence. It is likelier that problems might multiply. Always we fail, for we live in the anxiety of the creature; always we are finite, a fact that education has not rigorously faced. Even in an outrightly Christian college there would be campus politics, not to mention the encroachments of an alien world. But in the bond of the Commandment a college can be an eager pilgrim, not a prisoner—either of proud bricks, or of a passing generation, or of some implicit false assumption. Dürer's picture "Praying Hands" [33] can perhaps provide a symbol of a true school. The hands were those of Dürer's friend. Both were artists, but the friend gave himself to hard toil that Dürer might have first chance of art. The hands are therefore hardened and cannot again be an artist's hands. They betoken the world of toiling men, the community in which education is set. Dürer stands as symbol of the group privileged to live in school or college, whose study is made possible by the hard work of the world. The picture itself represents the love of the college for its community. The prayer is—what? "Thou shalt love the Lord thy God."

Chapter Three . . . . FAILURE

OUR AGE, DESPITE war's desolation, is apt to blink the fact of failure. The term "guilt consciousness" is for witness. As psychology uses the words, they imply morbid guilt, and there is such an obsession—as, for instance, in a daughter who covers her amply provoked hatred of her parents by an overconscientious sense of duty toward them, with consequent "guilt consciousness" when the duty is not fulfilled. But the fact that guilt can be morbid does not disprove real guilt: the word is in the language. The sense of guilt can be valid. In that instance we can hardly get rid of guilt by tinkering with the consciousness. Guilt can be evasive as well as morbid. Perhaps there is more evasive guilt than morbid guilt. The commonest evasion is through "transfer": we blame the government or communism, human nature or God, rather than ourselves. The psychologist knows that guilt is valid; for he assumes that his patient, except in cases where the patient is too weak in selfhood or is insane, can act on the new light that their consultation throws on hidden motives. Else why hold any conversation? The patient and the consultant are alike responsible men. The word "responsible" means capable and obligated to live in response. To what or whom? If a man is responsible for new light, he is presumably responsible if he chooses darkness.

I

C. E. M. Joad's recent recantation is more convincing than the slipperiness with which the term "guilt consciousness" is sometimes used. He tells us that he was accustomed to explain all failure as due to personal or social frustrations, but that when he contemplated a German concentration camp with its devilish and deliberate cruelties, he could not be satisfied with such an account.[1] He realized that frustrations were still a factor: Germany's defeat, poverty, and chaos brought a violent reaction. But a concentration camp revealed another ingredient: an outright wicked choice, willed nihilism, perverse cruelty, consent to demonism. Joad is skilled in logic, as his career in British agnosticism has brilliantly shown. So he followed to its rigorous conclusion the fact of demonism and man's consent to it, the fact of baleful seduction in our world and man's readiness to choose it. The conclusion was inescapable: If this darkness besets the human adventure, mankind is lost, unless from beyond man there is the alliance of a higher and holier power—unless God. Thus the title of Joad's book: *God and Evil.* The agnostic became a believer by a strange road, by confronting the bleak fact of man's failure.

Failure, if realistically faced, is seen to be paradoxical proof of hidden greatness. For only a creature intended for the heights can fall. The church has often failed to stress this fact, so its condemnations of sin have seemed only censoriousness. A man-eating tiger cannot be charged with murder. It knows no right and wrong, and therefore cannot fall. But a man can act earthily, and therefore is potentially of heaven. So if guilt is merely "guilt consciousness," because consciousness now and then gets out of order somewhat like a radio, psychology itself is only a poor "fixit shop," and human nature only an intricate mechanism of brain and bone. Such a conclusion, far from denying the value of true psychology, reveals the core of its value. A worm cannot fall; a bird can fall. To confess the fall of man is not to brand him a "worthless worm," but precisely to declare that his spirit has wings. Only man's shining awareness of the Great Commandment could ever brand him with insolvency. Failure is not due to our slowness to "get at the facts" or to "use them scientifically": only a shallow age could ever have accepted so shallow an explanation. Failure is *in* man. If we wished to add deep question to deep question, we might ask: Is darkness also in nature which breeds decay and death? That added question aside, failure, the mark of man's perversity, is the mark also of man's potential divinity. Thus the director of the Institute of Education in the University of London concludes that "Original Sin may be more than an outworn theological dogma after all." [2] Such realism confronts us with mystery: Why was the world thus made? But, then, there may be one or two items in the cosmos that our little minds can touch but cannot compass!

II

This fact of failure is written across education, perhaps even more than across some other endeavors, because education is more vulnerable to pride of the mind. A farmer cannot get too cocksure: he is too dependent on earth and sky. But a scientist, having built the manageable little world of his laboratory, and having there seen things come to pass at his bidding, with skyscrapers and airplanes as impressive proof, may easily assume that the world is his to control and that he can conquer sin and death as soon as he gets around to them. He does not see that his success is due partly to his contraction of his world. Raphael's "Madonna" could be quite satisfactorily explained if it were agreed beforehand that the only concern is the chemical constitution of pigment and canvas. So perhaps the failure of education is "naturally" worse than, let us say, that of a doctor who knows that he must at last lose every patient.

Who could deny the failure? There are thirty million pupils in our United States public schools alone, taught by upwards of a million teachers. The educational system, even though teachers and professors are culpably underpaid, costs a Midas fortune; and the teaching is reiterated and intense—thirty hours a week for ten to twenty school years. With what issue? Mark the cowardice of political life—the specious pleas, the vote catching, the cringing and cadging before special "interests." Mark the cult of success—a childish mixture of cash, gadgets, and ostentation. Mark the veiled mendacity of much of our advertising, its incredible braggadocio, its appeal to low motive ("Buy a car that your neighbor will envy"), its thinly disguised greed. Mark the panacea of "preparedness," ever offered as final gospel, ever disproved, with worst disaster falling on nations best prepared. Mark the radio as symbol of our civilization—money itch stealing the air, giveaway programs that should affront the intelligence of a grade school, the priesthood of announcers who with unction or simulated excitement peddle somebody's spaghetti or cigarettes as items of eternal salvation. Let us hope that the visitor from Mars does not arrive. We might be put to shame even by him. "Whom the gods would destroy they first make mad."

Is education responsible? Only in its measure. Perhaps

the church has more grievously failed. All vocations are chargeable with failure. But education has had these men hour on hour, day on day, year on year; and education has taught them neither sober worth nor genuine joy. Henry P. Van Dusen quotes two students. One wrote:

> It might be expected that in acquiring a liberal education, a group of young men might find ideas and ideals to which they could cling with courage and conviction. But . . . perhaps nowhere is there so much lip service paid to democratic ideals and so little stern devotion . . . as in the American colleges.

The other wrote:

> What have we been taught to revere? When *our elders* refer to eternal verities, absolutist ethics, *we* are likely to recall the lesson your instructors in sociology have driven home—that morals are relative to time and place, and what is good in one society is bad in another . . . that men create gods in their own image. . . . We, the young, are the American tragedy.[3]

Though we allow for the fact that young people are somewhat like preachers who pour oil on pulpit angers to see how merrily they may burn, the bill of indictment can hardly be disproved. Some colleges have bought athletes, to gather crowds, to amass money, to—do what? Perhaps they do not know. If their goal is worthy, surely a college should be aware that it cannot find an eastern window by moving west.

The attempt of education to wash its hands of world chaos is further token of failure. I do not judge. Yet I wonder and wonder as research men say in effect: "It is no business of mine if greedy men exploit my findings for drab gain, or violent men turn them to man's destruction." It *is* their business, if only because greed and violence now threaten research. The explosions come nearer and nearer to the laboratory: the next bomb may destroy the building and the research. No man can forswear the terms of his manhood: he is always a responsible man. If a man is reasonably sure that his invention will be used destructively, should he seek to perfect it? Perhaps no man knows the answer. But all men should know and confront the question. Suppose the answer is that research should continue, at whatever risk. The research man is then under more instant obligation to do all he can to guarantee the right use of his findings. He cannot claim immunity because he is in education: the calling lays on him a more urgent debt.

III

There is no joy in drawing this indictment. When any writer becomes judge, he himself is under heavier judgment; for has not Jesus said, "If you were blind, you would have no guilt; but now that you say, 'We see,' your guilt remains"? [4] The bill of accusation is written only that we may ask what educators or any other group of men can do in failure. That question finds education astonishingly naïve. Some scientists (honor to them!) have suddenly realized that they *do* have responsibility for the common life, and have become earnest advocates of world government. Here I write with double care: I would not be misconstrued as opposing so worthy a plea, so inevitable a cause. Clearly some form of world government must come, by whatever intermediate steps, if our planet is to survive. What gives pause is the assumption behind the plea, namely this: world government is clearly indicated by reason, and people are reasonable beings; and therefore if we show them this reasonableness, they will pronto establish a reasonable world. Such an assumption cannot bear scrutiny. Sometimes the assumption is even more naïve: world government will solve all ills. One is reminded of the village which tried to solve the problem of its impure water supply by installing a new pump. When a speaker in my church had pleaded eloquently for world government, a little lady with a penchant for asking awkward but crucial questions inquired disarmingly: "Will the speaker please tell us what he proposes to do about human nature?" Education has been naïve about human nature. The plea for world government is still valid and urgent, provided it is coupled with a knowledge of what to do about human nature.

"But *aren't* people reasonable beings?" The educator

sometimes asks the question with impatience; for when education becomes dominantly scientific, working only in its ponderable world, it is at a loss before the imponderables of human behavior. The answer is that people *are* rational, but that their rationalism is always under threat from irrationalism both within and beyond themselves. So Jesus said of the irrationalism that arrested Him in the tragic Garden of Gethsemane: "This is your hour, and the power of darkness." [5] How *could* Germany sell out to the cheap megalomania of a Hitler? Some of us knew its professors and played tennis against its student teams. We have in America thousands of fine folk from Germany. They would never tolerate a pogrom or a concentration camp. The steps of descent, however inexplicable, are easy to trace: the psychology of defeat, then the hopelessness of political chaos and economic poverty, then the "transfer" which made the Versailles Treaty the scapegoat for all ills, then the appeal to "blood and race," then the malign irrationalism which could have said

> Farewell remorse! All good to me is lost;
> Evil, be thou my Good.[6]

Hitler made deliberate appeal from reason to passion:

> All the great movements of history are volcanic eruptions of passions and spiritual sensations provoked either by the

cruel Goddess of Misery or by the torch of speech thrown to the masses. Only a storm of burning passion can change the destinies of a people.[7]

Psychology has only rediscovered what the Bible long ago told: there is an irrational subconscious, a malign and combustible demonism below the floor of life. Secular education has no defense against it. In Germany education did not oppose it, but rather made common cause with it, or continued to invite it by the vacuum of an arid scientism. So German education almost literally went up in smoke.

It is not enough to appeal to reason. No slogan is more vulnerable than the bromidic "What we need is more education." Education like that in Germany? Or like that in America when Huey Long, exploiting a time of depression, almost became our own Hitler? Education must ask what can be done about the subliminal irrationalism which besets human nature and which human nature invites. To say that we shall be all right "when once we get at the facts" is childishness. Germany had trillions of facts, but was not all right. What can be done about failure? Perhaps there is nothing that *we* can do, except in response to Salvation. No human power can purge away the poisons of the past, yet they must be purged from both the racial stream and the individual memory. No human power can cleanse history. Would any reader like to try, starting, let us say, with the bomb that fell on Hiroshima? Man's pilgrimage is a one-way journey. He cannot go back. Even if he could, the evil deed which he might resolve to purify has now spread like ink in a river; and even if he could overtake all that stain, the only will he would have for the task of cleansing would be his own poisoned will. So the slogan "Let us get at the facts and apply our reason" is precisely like saying of blind eyes and a broken arm, "Let us see our objective clearly and strike a mighty blow." All of which means that the difficulty is *in us*. "The evil which I would not, that I do." [8]

IV

Dimly we recognize the problem. Sometimes we are almost ready to confess our helplessness. But it is too hard a confession, especially for men surrounded by "the triumphs of science." So we seek escape through a romantic doctrine of progress. Mark the word "escape." It would be poetic justice in very truth if it were found that science and business, not religion, are the escape! Religion, except in some temporary eras when it has been tempted by poorly based optimisms, has been realistic about the twin facts of demonism and death. Consider the secularist's "progress." Now he finds that indeterminism is in the very quanta; now he is not sure even that "progress" can be transmitted from generation to generation. But he continues to believe. Unhappily for the belief, each generation dies: the road of "progress" is made of ground-up skulls. What of those in the midmost of the journey? Not much progress for them! Therefore what of us? Our progress is only the last big meal as a man goes to the electric chair. The real beneficiaries of "progress" are those who may live in a brief paradise at the end of history. Why should all other men be the coral reef, composed of generations of myriad dead insects, on which some ultimate generation can plant its garden? But even they, the blest fruition of "progress," are under shadow; for our planet, by dissipation of radioactive energy or some other cause, may be destroyed or become a slag heap like the moon. So "progress," the hope to which education has been dedicated whenever it has allowed itself any dedication, proves to be a road of ground-up skulls leading to oblivion. Begging the educator's pardon, some of us would prefer to name it the degradation of man and the blaspheming of God. Perhaps our doctrine of "progress" has been only a flight from reality.

But we must bar entrance to any such doubt. We cannot bear to see our dreamworld shattered. So, like many another suicide, we smash the real world and yield to the death wish and defiance. Or, with the rubble of world wars before our eyes, we still insist that all we need is scientific clarity. Arnold S. Nash has quoted John Dewey in just such insistence on exploded hopes: "That coercion and oppression on a large scale exist no honest person could deny. But these things are not the product of science and technology." [9] Therefore we must labor the more earnestly "with the use of all the resources which scientific material and the experimental method now put at our disposal." But coercion and oppression *are* "the product" of *men engaged in* "science and technology." Perhaps only one thing is more credulous than this refusal to face facts, namely, the readiness of thousands to join the refusal. We must admit that in initial instance any realism concerning human nature aids and abets human doubt and even brings despair. The Great Commandment, laid on men of poisoned nature, is impossible; and therefore its initial gift may be a sense of failure and remorse. Then men are tempted, unless they see the mutuality of the word "love" between God and men, to the defiance and death wish that mark our generation.

But true faith neither seeks escape in romantic doctrines of "progress" nor rushes from despair into nihilism. It says rather: "We are under holy command which, being holy, cannot be content with destroying us." Therefore the agelong prayer: "Forsake not the works of thine own hands." [10] Realism, leading on from despair to faith, is the road of salvation; for faith also is the gift of God and is always under His beckonings. But woe betide the generation that refuses the realism and says smilingly, "We must get at the facts!"

Browning tells a story of a girl with long golden hair and a matching shiningness of soul.[11] When she died young, her death hardly seemed death, because manifestly she was marked for the angel choir. Her friends were almost relieved when she asked as her last wish that she might braid her hair: that proved she was still human. She was buried beneath the chancel of the church, the rightful resting place for one so close to God. But, says Browning, when years later her skeleton was found, there was a circle of gold coins round the skull: she had been a miser. Thus the problem of human nature with its holy yearning and its immemorial bias toward evil! The poem is a real "getting at the facts," for it asks what to do about the immemorial "lie" in man's nature.

> Why I deliver this horrible verse?
>   As the text of a sermon, which now I preach:
> Evil or good may be better or worse
>   In the human heart, but the mixture of each
> Is a marvel and a curse.
>
> The candid incline to surmise of late
>   That the Christian faith proves false, I find;
> For our Essays-and-Reviews' debate
>   Begins to tell on the public mind . . . :

I still, to suppose it true, for my part,
  See reasons and reasons; this, to begin:
'Tis the faith that launched point-blank her dart
  At the head of a lie–taught Original Sin,
The Corruption of Man's Heart.[12]

The "lie" is the perversity within us. It would not be perversity if we were not aware of God. There is "a mixture of each"; and if a man would find proper ground for education or aught else, he must, to begin with, confront the essential facts of human nature, not be content with that quite secondary range of facts which is readily available to his astigmatic eyes. Of course the realism with its consequent despair is, "to begin," only a starting point; for Christian faith, though it confronts despair, finds salvation at that chasm edge, or, rather, is there found of God's salvation. If a man must love God, yet cannot love God, the word "love" is still a mutuality: the commandment itself tells that God loves him. The Christian gospel holds that the Word of God's love "was made flesh, and dwelt among us," [13] thus making common cause with man's need. Such a gospel comes to terms with *essential* facts.

Paul dared to declare the "curse of the law," [14] a curiously violent way for any man, especially a Christian, to write of the Great Commandment in its Old Testament setting. Yet the law does provoke that violence, which in our time has become defiance and perhaps a death wish. Has any reader ever fully kept the Great Commandment? Does he think he *can* keep it? The luncheon-club cliché, "My religion is the Golden Rule," should leave sober-minded men aghast. *Can* anyone keep the Golden Rule? Religion is the only answer to the problem raised by ethics. Only God can fulfill in human life the pure demand of the Great Commandment. Only God can cleanse history. Perhaps not even God can work that catharsis of man's pilgrimage except as He enters it with inevitable suffering. For how otherwise can we see God at work and consent to the cure? Tragedy is catharsis, as Greek drama well knew. Perhaps only the contemplation of an infinite Tragedy can cleanse away the "sins of the whole world." [15] "Christ hath redeemed us from the curse of the law, being made a curse for us," [16] so that now love for Him in response to His prior love for us is "the fulfilling of the law." [17] Thus the Cross is indeed the crux of history, the deed by which the dimension of the heavenly cuts into the broken and infected dimension of the earthly to redeem it. Let any reader compare the probing and profundity of such an interpretation of life with our shallow scientism or our romantically false "progress," and he will wonder how our generation could have been so self-deceived. He will wonder also how the present crisis in education could have been so long postponed.

He will know that education also, with all man's works, must be built on the Faith.

V

These are high mysteries, not easily made plain, especially to men who see through eyes dimmed by a false theory of "knowledge." Jesus made truth plain through stories. Dare we attempt an allegory? It will lag the whole horizon's distance behind His stories. It will be a paper flower compared with blue gentians on a lakeshore. Yet it may gather some hint of truth from Him. So this:

AN ALLEGORY

THE CROSS AND THE GREAT COMMANDMENT

Once upon a time there was a town called Earth. It was shadowed yet sheltered by a mountain that seemed to cleave the sky. High on the mountain was an alabaster city, built on a sheer precipice of rock, and its name was the City of the Great Commandment. Often the Earth-people tried to climb that height, for the City was fair to see, though almost dismaying in its beauty. By day it trembled in a green mist, as if decked with trees; by night it glimmered in myriad lights. But some pride or folly always tripped the climbers, so they slid back and seemed doomed to remain in Earth. They had eyes to see and hearts to yearn, but no strength to scale the height. The City of the Great Commandment seemed mockery even while it shone in welcome.

So the Earth-folk moved along drab streets and talked often of the shining City. Some said, "It is better to see, even if we cannot climb, than to be blind." But others answered with tears, "Why better if we can never attain? The City reminds us of our failures, mocks our hopes, and brings us to despair." There were rebel spirits who cried out bitterly: "Why should a man live in remorse? The City makes impossible demands. What is height or depth, good or evil? We would destroy the City if we could!" The gentler folk of Earth hardly knew what to answer. They saw no hope of climbing above Earth, but they could not take their eyes from the mountain that wore a shining City as though it were a pearl. After dark they would pray: "Lord of the City, save us!" Then the strength of the mountain entered into them, but they were still condemned to live on the plain.

The scientists and builders in the town grew clever with brick and steel. They determined to build a tower high as the City-rock. But every tower collapsed before it reached that height. The sands of Earth were filled with the ruins. Then the clever ones contrived airplanes that carried bombs. They vowed to subdue the City by force. But a Voice like thundering oceans rolled through the chasms of the mountain: "Thou shalt love the Lord thy God, and thy neighbour as thyself. These machines are made in pride, not love. You cannot bomb your way into the Great Commandment." The airplanes crashed into each other, and the streets of Earth ran with blood. But the City was untouched. That night, as lightning flashed about the precipice, the City glistened like a tear. Then still cleverer men arose in Earth who asked, "How do you know there *is* mountain or a City? They are but projections of the mind to comfort man in his mortality. Ideals are only chemistry. Earth can be comfortable while we live, and death is death." But Earth could not forget the City. Through every window they saw its grandeur or its shadow. From its lower slopes they cut wood and quarried stone to build their homes. From its glaciers came streams and cooling winds to give surcease in summer heat, while in winter's storms the mountain's bulk was like a man's strong shoulder to a child. Besides, the folk of Earth found that they could not even trade without some bond of honor, and the City spoke to them of the bond of honor. So the rebels shook their fists, but wistful men asked, "Does the Lord of the City see us? Has He pity for our failure?"

One day the rumor ran that a Man living in a poor street of Earth had come there from the City of the Great Commandment. Most people laughed aloud at the idea. "Hasn't he a name like our name, Joshua, Jesus?"

they asked. One man said, "I work in the same carpenter shop. Yesterday he cut his finger, and it bled with blood like my blood. He would have bled to death if we had not stanched the flow. He is not from the mountain!" Yet there was something strange about the Man. He had no regrets. There were no shadows in His eyes. He could read His neighbor's secret thoughts: men shrank back, and yet were drawn. He was living conscience, yet passing kind. His words took people off guard. He would say to a rich man, "Why do you carry that weight? No wonder you cannot climb." Then just when people were ready to brand him demagogue, He would overtake a poor man on the road and say, "Do not pity yourself. Blessed are the poor: they know their need of God." One day He turned suddenly to a fleshly man and said: "Trying to clutch an earthly paradise? Paradise is up the mountain. Is love your word, or lust?"

Ever and again His eyes were lifted to the City. The peace and strength of it were in His face. The cooling breeze and the life-giving streams were in His deeds. Some people came to Him praying, "Save me from the Earth-life!" and He seemed to draw the sting of evil. They felt that with Him to guide they yet could climb the mountain. But the rebel spirits hated Him as darkness hates the light. They said, "He never knew the City, but the City's curse is on Him, for He fills us with senseless remorse and brings despair. Who could keep His impossible commands?" One of them asked Him, "What is truth?" as if to say, "There are dividends in money shrewdness, but none in truth."

Yet for some strange reason they envied Him even while hating Him. So they resolved to kill Him. Suddenly they swirled about Him, a lynching mob. "Nail Him high!" a voice cried. "Let us see if His City will save Him!" So at the edge of town on a black nub of land they killed Him. Darkness covered the white City though it was yet day, and one sword of lightning split the sky. As He died He turned His face to the mountain and prayed, "Father, forgive them; for they know not what they do." [18]

He should have been forgotten. The rebel souls in Earth said His death was good riddance. They quoted scripture, as the devil can do to suit his purpose: "Cursed is every one that hangeth on a tree." [19] They were sure that the curse had blotted out His name. But He was not forgotten. That night a group of His friends met and tried to ease their sorrow by remembering Him. They recalled this tenderness He had spoken and that courage He had shown.

The philosopher said: "Earth was no fit place for Him. He was far better than most of us, yet the victim of evil like all men. Why should we expect the City to visit our dull plain?"

The pessimist had a darker word: "Yes, in every man

there are good and evil, with never an end to the conflict. Even a saint in a desert hears a demon whisper in his ear. Every war brings not peace, but only worse war. Nothing can save man from the cleft in his own nature. That is why the Stranger was hung on a gallows."

But a woman said, "I know He forgave me. How do I know? How do I know spring water after thirst? How do I know home after the weary road?"

And a man spoke: "He forgave me too, though I have grabbed and grafted all my life. Only God can forgive, for our sins are against Him at last, and pardon is His right and grace. Only God can mend the broken past. Surely God was in Him! Surely He came from the mountain!"

The philosopher answered quickly: "But if God came, He would suffer. Can you imagine how a God-man from the mountain would suffer in this greedy town? He could not bear it. He would die of a broken heart."

"He did die," the woman said. "He did suffer. He suffered as He walked our streets. He suffered as He died. I watched Him at the end, and it seemed like the agony of God. Perhaps we needed it, for are we ever cleansed except by sight of tragic sorrow?"

The pessimist spoke the final word: "He died, and He is dead."

So they wept silently and at midnight groped their way home. Sadness is a drug: soon they fell on hopeless sleep.

But the next day they could not forget. The four met in the market place. The forgiven woman said: "When I was a child, my mother sucked a bee sting from my hand, and I feared she would die. Jesus sucked the poison from my heart, and perhaps that is why He died."

The forgiven man said: "Once in a war I was captured, and every tenth man was condemned to be shot because of atrocities from our side. A friend offered to take my name and number, because he was alone and I had wife and child. So he would have done had we not all been rescued. A man can take another man's name, but not his nature, not his failures. Yet I felt that Jesus took my nature and gave me His spirit for my guilty blunders. Surely God was in Him!"

The pessimist said again: "But He died and is dead."

"Yes," said the philosopher, "if He had not died, you might have had the one story of all history: God entering time to redeem its brokenness. What a faith if He had not died!"

The City on the mountain seemed unmoved. Perhaps there was unwonted quietness, as if history had come to a stop, but there was no other sign. Nobody tried to climb, or wished to try. "Thou shalt love the Lord thy God, and thy neighbour as thyself"? The mountain was much

> too high for man's upreaching,
> Coldly sublime, intolerably just.[20]

Earth was here, all too earthy; the City was there, all too white and far.

The third day came, tremulous with dawn. The rebels had left the Cross standing, to warn the next fool who trusted soul instead of sense. The sun climbed the sky. Why was the Cross squarely between the sunrise and the mountain, so that the shadow of the Cross was printed on that wall of rock? Why should the alabaster City be set like a jewel just where the crossbeam cut the upright? The forgiven woman came running in ridiculous joy: "He is not dead! How do I know? How do I know the thrust of conscience in dark temptation? How do I know daybreak after a night of tears? Last night I was afraid: now I have no fear!"

The forgiven man came running: "He is not dead. I saw Him. He spoke to me in words better than speaking. Every common thing was edged with light brighter than light. He is risen from the dead!"

The rebels came running, for they had seen the shadow of the Cross printed on the mountainside. "The mark of our deed is on the whole earth and sky!" they said. "It cannot be, lest some curse come on us, lest some worse folly be fastened on foolish men!" So they broke the Cross close to the ground. But the shadow on the mountain was not broken. The shadow did not move. It shone there in somber glory, the foot of it in a town called Earth, the center of it in the City of the Great Commandment, the top of it in heaven. Nay, it seemed to the folk of Earth, as they stood looking, that the Cross on the mountain had become a pathway. "See them there!" they cried. Shadowy folk, souls of Earth, were climbing. No, not climbing: they were reaching upward in pained yet radiant longing, and angel hands reached down to lift them. Pilgrims who kept that path could climb—or be lifted. Shining ones came to meet them: the Great Commandment stooped to Earth.

The next day the pessimist and the philosopher met. "Another dream," said the pessimist, "a fiction from man's loneliness, easily understood, not to be condemned, yet false."

But the philosopher was troubled. "Fiction?" he asked. "Are you sure? They did not expect Him to rise: by our own law He was accursed. They are convinced they saw Him, and they are too honest to contrive a lie. Besides, why should they wish to recover *Jesus* by a *lie* when always He spoke truth? Nay, why should they wish His return? It would be too vast a demand. If He *has* come, no man may live an Earth-bound life. I do not understand it." He walked out to the dark nub of land when evening came, his thoughts more deeply troubled, but troubled as great music troubles the soul. He spoke with himself: "I said that if He had not died, He would have been history's Event. Newness in every event: but what newness in Him if He is not dead! Beyond doubt He touched a primal awe. If He has not died, because God cannot die, then we have seen in Him—who but the great God Himself, come to mend the brokenness of time, binding us forever with Himself! Now they say He has not died. They did not expect Him to return. They could not wish it: it is too vast a revolution, too great a rapture, too stern a command. Besides, they are honest folk: they are not crooks. If only I could understand!" He was sorely troubled, for a philosopher must understand. It is hard for him to become a child in spirit. It is hard for him to make the leap of faith.

He resolved that he would wait there until darkness came. Then, he thought, the shadow of the Cross would be swallowed up in darkness. Then men would soon forget that Jesus ever came to earth. Then philosophers would not be ambushed by new events with their trouble of mind. So he waited while darkness fell. But the shadow was not lost: it shone there, a luminous shadow, a pathway of golden light! The climbing men were now dark against the pathway. Climbing? Lifted, rather, for angel hands reached down to them. The philosopher fell on his knees and prayed: "Now lettest thou thy servant depart in peace . . . ; for mine eyes have seen thy salvation."[21] He had not known the pessimist had been watching with him. Absorbed, he had thought himself alone. But now as he knelt on a black nub of land, he felt the elbow of another kneeling man.

Incredibly he heard that sad voice, trembling now in a somber joy: "Lord, I believe; help thou mine unbelief." [22]

VI

Let the story stand. Let us return to the dull query and rejoinder in which books on education are supposed to be written. Little has been said in these pages about courses in religion. They help, and win our gratitude. They build at least a footbridge, however precarious, between church and school, between reverence and knowledge. It is an augury of hope that many a college has restored to its curriculum the story of man's agelong response to God's seeking. The difficulties implied in the comment, "But there are so many religions, and so many sharp cleavages even in the Christian Church," have been overstated. The college teaches rival theories of economics and government, and finds in the study of differences a clearer road to truth. This barrier, the rivalry of faiths, has not only been exaggerated; in part it has been overcome, for even in some state universities methods have been found for teaching religion.[23] The change, moreover, is apparently winning student welcome. But this book does not explore such methods because, whatever our gratitude for them, they are not the main issue. In fact they may distract from the main issue. Such courses are usually optional, and therefore encourage false notions, for they say to the student in effect: "Religion is a necktie, so choose the color you prefer, unless you would rather meet life in the more casual sport shirt." But religion is not a necktie: it is the main artery of a man's neck. It is all or nothing. It is a life commitment. Our contention in these pages is that every man lives by faith, that the cult of "objective truth" is rife with hidden false assumptions, and that the crisis in education will deepen into a "time disconsolate" unless we return to a true faith. Religion cannot be compartmentalized into courses: it must be *all through* education, or it is not religion.

Little has been said here of difficulties occasioned by our doctrine of "the separation of church and state." The doctrine needs rethinking. The founding fathers never intended that the state, including education, should be godless. On the contrary, they intended that all life should be godly. They saw that the church, becoming dominant, falls into coercions—such are the poisons of egocentrism—and they saw that the state, becoming dominant, starts inquisitions and persecutions of its own; therefore they decreed a wise separation of function wherein the inevitable tensions between church and state might be reduced. They saw also the dangers from compulsive sectarianism, and knew that the atheist's conscience also must be honored. But in all this they never even remotely favored a godlessness.[24] The National

Council of Independent Schools, not a source biased toward religion, is plainly right in its declaration:

> The tradition of American education derives from faith in God, faith in man, and the ideal of the widest educational opportunities for all. The disestablishment of churches was not intended to interfere with the faith of the people of the United States in a Supreme Being. When the country was founded, it was written into law and established in custom that, while there was to be separation between the powers of the State and those of churches, and while each American was to be protected from compulsory worship with any sect or creed, and while the right of any man to dissent according to his conscience was guaranteed, the reliance on God and trust in Him, by any believer, were to be recognized and perpetuated. Thus the source of our ultimate security and unity is an understanding of man's position in relation to eternal reality and participation in the resources of faith. This is the spiritual heritage to which our children are entitled.[25]

A recent decision of the Supreme Court,[26] while tender toward the right of infrequent atheistic conscience, tramples on the convictions of hosts of people who hold, however tenuously, to the faith. It almost penalizes the teaching of religion in schools and colleges. It should be revoked by public opinion issuing in new legislation concordant with the intention of our Constitution.

But the primary concern of this book is not with such

matters, for they are not the primary concern. This book pleads that education has had a faith while pretending to cleave only to "objective fact," that these implicit assumptions cannot bear scrutiny, and that we must therefore return to the faith in which alone our race has found a wellspring of life. "Return" does not mean setting back the clock (as if man ever could, or as if that silly phrase had much value), nor does it mean forswearing the rigor and the blessings which scientific thought has brought us. It means rather carrying that rigor to its conclusion—to see that the vague assumptions of "scientism" cannot bear scrutiny. This chapter is more particularly concerned with the issue of failure. Sir Walter Moberly has summarized the failure when he says of students that "under the guise of academic neutrality they are subtly conditioned to unthinking acquiescence in the . . . *status quo* and in a secularism on which they have never seriously reflected. . . . Fundamentally they are uneducated." [27] What to do with failure? It is in the past, and the past for human beings is past. The failure is willed, rooted in human pride, and its bane now poisons all life. Because the "lie" is in the will, the instrument of cure is itself diseased, unless—God. Without faith in redemption we are under sentence of death, or, worse, under what Francis Thompson called "sentence of life." [28] But if there is a Cross, and thereby a living pathway on the mountain, and angel hands as well as human climbing . . .

Education finds it hard to avow such a faith, not because the faith is unintelligent (for faith in Christ is surely not less intelligent in this broken era than faith in "progress"), but because it requires confession of helplessness, or, rather, a confession that God has made us for Himself and that we "find no rest until we rest in" [29] Him. How hard it is to confront the fact that our brilliant research, with all its drugs and radar, cannot heal man's spirit! How hard to admit that mind itself, apart from God, is cankered by mortal pride, and that we must therefore say at last of all our skills:

> We but teach
> Bloody instructions, which, being taught, return
> To plague the inventor.[30]

The school should not become the church, though quite conceivably it was an unhappy juncture that took education from the church to assign it to the state, but the bond must be kept between school and church. Assuredly the school must be grounded in worship. What other ground, as men seriously confront the fact and meaning of failure?

The Cross is the ground plan. The vertical line is a ladder set from heaven to earth, such as Jacob saw [31] and Christ fulfilled: "Thou shalt love the Lord thy God."

Granted that vertical loyalty, a crossbeam can then be securely fastened: "Thou shalt love thy neighbour as thyself." Duke University is built on the lines of a great cross, in memory of another Cross. Every college must so be built if it would stand. The top of the cross in Duke University is a chapel. There men bring their straining thought, infected by self-centered desires as in all men, to the cleansing and hope of worship. There they may know beyond all cavil and gainsaying that our life on earth is not a bagatelle or a trouble of ants, but personal worth held in the brooding of eternal Love. A church near Broadway printed a plain cross on a white background and underneath inscribed the title of a clever, but twisted and ephemeral, play then having its Broadway "run"—*Design for Living*.[32] If the Cross is the design for living, a Givenness to which we may therefore respond, a Love winning our answering love, it is the design also for education.

Chapter Four . . . . DESTINY

THE trout fisherman walking through a backwoods valley gazed incredulously on a house that seemed to have sprung from the ground. An elderly woman appeared at the door. "Come and see it. My sons from Detroit built it in a week end." It was not finished: the interior walls were skeletons, with two-by-fours for bones. "This is where the stove will go." In each room she supplied imaginary furniture. Yet the substance of the house had been built in a week end.

But other houses are not so quickly built. How long will it take to build the Great Commandment in our earth? "Thou shalt love the Lord thy God . . . and thy neighbour." But we hardly know our neighbor in a lifetime, let alone learn to love him. Much less do we know and learn to love God. Man, with only temporal powers, is under an eternal demand; and his equipment is an unfledged mind and a few turns of the clock. It is as if someone had said: "Here are a hundred bricks: build a cathedral in a week end." Love God and our neighbor? A man hardly begins, stumbling in the attempt, when death taps him on the shoulder.

I

Few people face that issue. We Americans in particular prefer to live as if we would never die. So we are usually in a hurry, inwardly driven by a knowledge of death that we try to repress. Meanwhile we boast of "progress," which proves on examination to be only a road of skulls leading to planetary disintegration. Education shares this evasive romanticism. How many colleges have acknowledged in their curriculum the inescapable finitude of man's mind? The prospectus invites the student to "the discovery of truth." The phrase itself puts the cart before the horse, for we are creatures, and therefore truth must discover us. In any event no man can discover truth in the narrow limits of this life. What the prospectus should say is: "Come and learn that you cannot discover truth." The proposal is made in soberness, not in whimsy; for if it were adopted, students might inquire about the horizons of life, and colleges might become homes of wisdom instead of bustling cafeterias of information. So the reader is invited to an exercise in realism, along the lines of the motto inscribed on a friend's paperweight: "Knowledge is proud she knows so much; wisdom is humble she knows no more."

Consider the fact that all knowledge is conditioned by its generation. It is stained by its time. Struggle as it may, it is under duress to its date. In an agrarian age economics of "supply and demand" was passably true, but it is untrue, or only partly true, in a planet of wars and machines when all physical frontiers are merging into a world-wide culture. Nowadays economics is almost driven to postulate other "laws," such as "security" and "satisfaction." A book like *Business Adrift*,[1] in which a Harvard professor of economics confessed that he and his colleagues must now seek new criteria, marked the change. But what made the change? A changing world, induced in part by the initiatives of man's mind, but a world nevertheless which no man could clearly foresee. There are illustrations in every area of knowledge. Drama was one thing in Shakespeare's time in the Globe Theater; it is another in our "psychological era" on Broadway. We think we think, and then fashion the world to our thinking, but it is perhaps just as true to say that the world kicks us in the ribs to make us think. Time is change, and change tinctures all thinking with its dyes, and what is "true" in one generation is almost untrue in the next. There is a more mysterious fact: time breeds decay. The "pathetic fallacy" might say that time is cursed by "original sin": the immense reptiles of eighty million years ago were afflicted by cancer. But that pondering would carry us into too deep waters. Let us be content with a milder fact, namely, that truth is partially relative to its generation. If another instance is required: the Mayflower on its next trip carried slaves, and in that slave trade there was another vessel called "Jesus." Some of *our* so-called truths may likewise appall our posterity.

Consider the allied fact that as we advance in knowledge, or hope we advance, the goal of knowledge recedes. Every mystery solved is still not solved, for it arouses six other mysteries from sleep. Astronomy moved from a sun-centered world to a radioactive universe, to a doctrine of relativity, to–? Cosmic space is itself a bafflement, for it may turn out to be only another form of cosmic time. Bible study provides further instance, if any is needed. We used to think that the Bible was dictated infallibly, until the Bible itself refuted the notion, as the stars themselves refuted a pre-Copernican astronomy. We might have guessed that a man turned into a dictaphone would be mechanized rather than inspired, and that a God who employed a man as if he were a machine would be a tyrant rather than God. But man's insights are slow at best. In the new view of the Bible we were still sure of some facts, so we imagined. We believed confidently that Matthew, let us say, wrote the first Gospel. But then we found that Matthew was indebted to Mark, even to the extent of what we would call plagiarism, though a plagiarism which in those days was an accepted literary method. Now we know that Matthew is probably a generation later than Mark, and that all the Gospels, far from being simple "lives of Jesus" in which the Church was born, are themselves in part a golden harvest from the life of the Church. This now accepted postulate seems clear gain. But it brings other questions such as these: Who, then, was Matthew? How much is his Gospel colored by conditions in the church from which he wrote? If the Gospel was written for catechumens, as now seems almost sure, how much has the autograph been modified to meet their powers of understanding?

This fact that the goal of knowledge seems to recede as time advances raises even profounder queries, such as that concerning the nature of time itself. Perhaps we should say that time stands still while we move in time. Perhaps the more accurate phrase would be that time recedes. We do not know: the space-time continuum is a great mystery. At any rate we are like stage-horses in our so-called knowledge: we have to run as fast as we can to stay where we are. The poet may have been accurate, not merely poetic, in his description of our human days:

> Life, like a dome of many-coloured glass,
> Stains the white radiance of Eternity.[2]

All our knowledge may be only the exploration of a domed house. Truth may be always beyond the windows of mortality, yet forever shining through them. Perhaps faith, sitting at the window, has a better verity than our poor interior explorations, even though the window is colored and partly opaque. Science, busily and usefully itemizing the house, cries, "I have found the truth"; faith, gazing through the window, answers, "I am found of Him, but His ways are past finding out." [3] Our knowledge is relative. Our "facts" are always infected with finitude. It is a somewhat appalling conceit that any college should invite its students to "the discovery of truth."

At risk of being called an unconscionable pest, I must point to another proof of the shortness of man's mind. This: the multitude of "facts" is already beyond us. How many facts are there in *The Encyclopaedia Britannica?* But that is only a brief compendium. How many facts would there be if an exhaustive encyclopaedia were written for each department of human knowledge? In astronomy or economics alone there are millions of facts. Then how long must we continue to amass facts? Already they are far more than we can number, let alone marshal, let alone understand and interpret. We are like a greedy man who does not know how much he owns in investments and property, still less what to do with them. Education should not evade this issue, for education too long has been like the man crying, "When we find a large enough building supply-depot, we shall be at home."

The man meanwhile gathers more and more supplies until there is supply-depot to the horizon on every side; yet still he has no home, but only a greedy homelessness. How long are we supposed to go on gathering facts? Perhaps we must answer that man's mind must strain and ever strain to know. But by what principle and for what purpose? Browning's Grammarian found a lifetime too short for the study of a few Greek participles:

> So, with the throttling hands of death at strife,
> Ground he at grammar;
> Still, through the rattle, parts of speech were rife:
> While he could stammer
> He settled *Hoti's* business—! let it be—
> Properly based *Oun*—
> Gave us the doctrine of the enclitic *De*,
> Dead from the waist down.[4]

Such is the pathos of all human knowledge. The absent-minded professor gets that way because he has so little time to learn even an iota of all there is to learn, and because memory is too frail to carry even a minor cargo of facts. Our knowledge is now so multifarious and so specialized as to be beyond *educational* synthesis. Not even Plato's seventy "airy burgomasters," meditating constantly on their secluded mountaintop,[5] could even correlate, let alone "inwardly digest," our myriad diet of facts. Should we say that only faith in control of avaricious mind can give interpretation? Meanwhile each specialist, locked in his own study, wears blinders; and therefore we have the "psychological fallacy" and the "scientific fallacy" and the "pathetic fallacy." Yet colleges invite the student to "the discovery of truth." They would be wiser to invite him to pray that the college may someday have a sense of humor.

II

Of course Browning's Grammarian, though "dead from the waist down" while struggling to master two or three fragments of total knowledge, was not to be pitied, for he had a faith. He believed in God and in eternal life, and therefore was not overborne by an avalanche of facts. Soon he would be in another dimension, beyond the "dome of many-coloured glass." So he studied in quiet joy, not in greedy desperation or mortal pathos:

> Others mistrust and say, "But time escapes:
>   Live now or never!"
> He said, "What's time? Leave Now for dogs and apes!
>   Man has Forever." [6]

Unless the Grammarian was right, knowledge is mockery; and the Great Commandment is mockery, a sky beckoning to wings caught in clay. Education must confront the problem of mortality or die in the attrition of an unconfessed despair. German scientism is the attrition, and Hitler the sign of despair.

Our modern evasions do not help us: they bear the brand of despair. A sneer like "pie in the sky by and by" is no good gift. It has its point, and the point is needed to puncture pretensions in the Church which forsake present duty to moon about future bliss. The bliss is very uncertain for those who try to evade the duty. Nevertheless the sneer makes no final sense. For if the universe is so unjust that it gives a man a hundred bricks and bids him build a cathedral in a week end, no resolve on our part to rear a juster world can win success. For the whole scheme of things is against us:

> The pillared firmament is rottenness,
> And earth's base built on stubble.[7]

In such a world the crusade for brotherhood is doomed before it begins. The sneer about "one world at a time" is likewise empty. A radicalist lecturer in Hyde Park, London, spotted in the crowd a man wearing a clerical collar and asked him: "Why don't you take one world at a time?" The preacher looked embarrassed and made no answer. So I, a brash youth, answered, "He can't, and you can't." The lecturer was about to turn on me when my college buddy intervened to ask: "Anybody ever die in your house?" The lecturer stopped, and then said bitterly: "That is hitting below the belt." He did not tell who had died. The question was not below the belt, but in the heart—where man's deepest life is lived. When death comes we cannot help wondering; and that wonder promptly makes us citizens of two worlds at a time, however tenuous our suffrage in that other world.

Other evasions are just as flimsy a contention. "Life can be beautiful"? Not if there is a dagger hidden in every bouquet that life hands us! Not if we are given a hundred bricks and told to build a cathedral! Not if the demon always mocks the angel! Not if every crusade of brotherhood is belied by the world itself! Not if every grammarian is of such frail years that even a Greek participle laughs at his resolve to "know"! Education is confronted by the problem of destiny. Is there not a slippery character in Dickens who, wishing to rent his house, would say to some gullible prospective tenant that it had "an uninterrupted view across the street"? Perhaps education has offered students no better prospect, despite the grandiose invitation to "discover truth." The promise that "we shall live in the immortality of noble influence," whether true or untrue, is assuredly no promise. It begs all the questions with childish naïveté. Perhaps there is no influence without ongoing personality: have we any right to make the assumption? And what if the planet becomes extinct? And would anyone really wish to live in a world beset, with whatever education, by smells of the hosts of the dead? John S. Whale[8] has rightly shown the confusion in George Eliot's lines:

> Oh may I join the choir invisible
> Of those immortal dead who live again
> In minds made better by their presence.[9]

If that is the only life hereafter, there is no "choir," or even music or an organ. How can the "dead" be "immortal" if they are "dead"? How can they have a "presence"? How can we be sure that minds would be "better" living in a charnel house, even though the house might be suffused by a dim light?

There is this to be said for Christian faith: its hopes are substantial hopes, and it never romanticizes about death. It says bluntly in proper terror: "The last *enemy* to be destroyed is death." [10] In the onset of the terror it finds God, or, rather, is found of God. It says that the enemy has been overcome in Jesus Christ, in whom our best hopes, such as the hope that personality has a value worth keeping, are validated. He "hath brought life and immortality to light through the gospel." [11] That faith is worth examination, if only because it has bred the kind of character that has "stopped the mouths of lions." [12] Education, confronting destiny, must choose between a dull stoicism that sees nothing beyond death, or a romanticism which whistles in the dark a broken tune about the immortality of influence, or an outright Christian faith. So an inquiry into Christian faith has its place.

III

We do not ask if Christian faith is "true," for that word conjures up the processes of logic. Logic lives by a truth it must assume, and only so can it prove anything. We ask rather if there are certitudes by which faith in eternal life is justified. Faith in life eternal antedated Christ, at least in some vague form. Men have always believed in, or dimly hoped for, a life beyond death. Our sneers testify to our hope, even though only in denial. Christ "brought" it "to light" and life. His resurrection, together with His life and death, is therefore the nerve center of Christian faith. Can we honestly believe in His resurrection? The earliest books in the New Testament were written within thirty years of the Crucifixion. The witnesses, that is to say, were contemporaries of Jesus; and their reliability could be verified or disputed by other contemporaries. The first account chronologically is probably that in First Corinthians. In its simplicity it almost asks people to scrutinize it. "He appeared to Cephas, then to the twelve. Then he appeared to more than five hundred brethren at one time, most of whom are still alive, though some have fallen asleep. Then he appeared to James." [13] The word "appeared" is not embellished, but it implies that the initiative was with Jesus, that the experience had objectivity.

Probably they expected no such appearing. Afterward the Church found prophecies of the Resurrection in the words of Jesus, but beforehand a Jesus crucified meant a Jesus accursed. "His body shall not remain all night upon the tree, but thou shalt in any wise bury him that day; (for he that is hanged is accursed of God;) that thy land be not defiled, which the Lord thy God giveth thee." [14] It is even doubtful if they wished He might rise: a man accursed could bring no blessing. They mourned Him, but perhaps with no better hope than the Jewish Sheol, a shadowy land of half life to which (in Jewish thought) the dead went. This curse of the Crucifixion is ignored by slapdash theories which would have us believe that Paul and his friends draped Christianity, as a mystery cult, on the figure of a little-known Jewish rabbi.[15] Another fact steadily ignored is that the New Testament writers were resolved on honesty. They yearned to live in that same rigor of verity in which Jesus bade them live. A lie left them undone: a lie about Christ was blasphemy. "If Christ be not risen, . . . we are found false witnesses of God." [16] They shrank from such perfidy. The New Testament was not written by crooks or medicine men.

By worldly standards they had nothing to gain from their faith in the Resurrection. From the standpoint of comfort they would have been well advised to hush the story. They were ostracized in the markets, in some instances stripped of citizenship, and not a few of them sealed their testimony in their blood. How can any theory of "illusion" or "wishful thinking" stand against these facts? The men of the New Testament feared neither pain nor death, because they were sure that their Lord had risen from the dead. There are other facts as hard to by-pass or surmount. This fact: the Jewish Sabbath, bastioned worthily in worshiping centuries, yielded place to the Christian Sunday—the day on which He rose from the dead. This fact: the New Testament has no in memoriam note, but is written *because* "Christ . . . hath abolished death." [17] This fact: the Church came into being because of the Resurrection and abides despite both its own treacheries and the world's contumely or indifference. To try to account for this range of fact by speaking of "a vision conjured up by sorrow" or "a woman's hallucination" is as unconvincing as to say of the sunrise, "Someone must have struck a match."

Our minds are under the near deification of science. It is hard for us to believe in the Resurrection of Jesus because that event seems an exception to the "law" that all men are mortal. Perhaps there is no law, but rather a Divine "contingency"! We find it hard to think of Him as dead! We have not yet come to terms with the new science: contingency, not law, is now the solving word.

The newness in each event, not its likeness with other events, gives it distinctive character; for otherwise it would hardly be worth calling an event. That the world or any man should have come into being at all is miracle, not law. Christian faith is not alien from the doctrine of contingency. It has always avowed that in the midst of history there occurred *the* Event—the birth, death, and resurrection of Jesus Christ—and that therein God Himself spoke, and that His word is the "Great Divide" of human story. There is evidence for this faith, as I have tried to show. But there is no compulsive evidence: we are not spared the venture of faith. Meanwhile there is evidence enough of the bankruptcy of other faiths. Godlessness has run its course—into chaos. But Christ abides, in whom education can find deliverance from the blight of mortality.

IV

Can we tell more specifically the meaning of a Resurrection faith for education? There is assurance of pardon for failure, whether in education, business, or church. The Peter who at Pentecost confronted unafraid the mob which had clamored for Christ's death, and told them bluntly, "This Jesus, . . . you crucified and killed by the hands of lawless men," [18] was a changed man from the Peter who had cringed before a servant maid's challenge to his faith. By what power was he changed? By the event of the Resurrection, and not least because that event spelled the redemption of his denials. The worst that man could do at Calvary—the venom of leaders in the temple, the callousness of empire, the blood lust of the crowd, the gaping indifference of passers-by, the treachery of friends—was not enough to kill the Lord of life, in whom any penitent man can find pardon. Without faith in that renewing power who could rightly live? Not a teacher feeding eager youth the straw of "facts," nor a doctor dealing with folk as if they were but bodies, nor a preacher dulling the Good News by perfunctory sermons! Who can cleanse away the blot on Hiroshima? Everyone was to blame—scientists, warmongers in any land, politicians and those who elected them, and the common man making the common mind—but no one on earth can recall the bomb or summon the dead to life. Yet unless the blot be cleansed, with a million other blots, all earth becomes blot. If, as I have contended, education with its thin rationalism has no defense against a subliminal irrationalism, where is the defense? The Resurrection is sign of a structure of regnant grace over against the uprush of demonism. "Where sin abounded, grace did much more abound." [19] The Resurrection, not without the sacrifice at Calvary, won life from hate, violence, and all dullness. What other word is worth speaking in our convicted age?

There is mending also for the half-truths which education has taught as truths, the "verities" which one generation accepts and the next generation questions. Christ took the intention of a half-loyalty for the whole deed. "Ye are they which have continued with me in my [testings]." [20] They had not, but He received the will for the fulfillment. What of the theory of molecules so confidently taught but now disproved? What of evolutionary doctrines offered as an escalator of hope which now must yield to discussion of "contingents" and "emergents"? What of Bible teachings which Bible teachers, in the coming of fuller light, must now qualify or disown? What of a war fought for democracy which gave communism its start, and a second war which spread communism until now it threatens any deep freedom? Our intended good always proves partly false, a fact that may have prompted Wordsworth's prayer:

> The best of what we do and are,
> Just God, forgive! [21]

Our very knowledge issues in folly, and our projected "right" becomes the unwitting ally of wrong. No teacher can teach in that awareness unless he believes that God gathers the dissonance of man's shortsighted "truth" into His symphony. That gathering is precisely what happened at the Resurrection: even the blindness that thought Calvary was "a service to God" was turned to God's purpose and man's gain.

V

There are ventures as well as recoveries when education finds in the Great Commandment a radiant destiny beyond this life. That faith is a home from which the mind can pioneer and to which it can return for solace and renewal. The mind cannot live without a home. It cannot live in suspended judgment, for suspense cannot long be endured. Modern man has tried the suspense of believing nothing, and because suspense is soon unbearable, he has ended by believing almost anything:

> I believe without bother
> In This, That, and T'other;
>   Whatever is current, no matter.
> I believe in Success,
> And in Comfort no less;
>   I believe all the rest is but patter.[22]

That is, modern man has no home, but only a succession of rooms in cheap lodging houses. How can any man study in such homelessness? The mind, like any traveler, needs a compass and a fixed point of departure; and wherever the mind may go, it must establish a new home—in the ancient sanctities. The mind needs abidingness for its very pioneering. Otherwise it is precisely like the boy lost at the World's Fair. There were sciences enough in fascinating demonstration to content him; there were gadgets and amusements galore. But the lad was inconsolable: "I'm lost! I'm lost!" The angels, who have keener ears than men, have heard that cry of late from many a campus. Even a Columbus cannot journey without some Spain from which he gathers his resources. Christ is what God means by man, and what man means by the spirit and purpose of God—that faith can give a haven of return and a point of venture.

All of which means that we are not handed a hundred bricks and then told to build a cathedral in a week end. We are given enough material with which to start, and beyond time another dimension of opportunity. We cannot be slothful, but we need not hurry. "Now I know in part; but then shall I know even as all along I have been known." [23] We need not study or teach in the half frenzy of the Marquand hero of *So Little Time!*" [24] By the faith we are already in the new dimension, or at least we see where it cuts the dimension of our world; and we are sure, in an axiomatic persuasion from which logic also draws its life, that hereafter the new dimension will be the order and climate of our education. The Great Commandment is not mockery, but promise. An ultimate demand is laid on our poor temporal powers because we are destined for an ultimate life. The Great Commandment leads us to the opening of Plato's cave[25] and says: "Now make the cave decently homelike by means of this incoming light, and soon you shall journey into that wide-beckoning and shining land." Therefore the Grammarian[26] still pursued his studies and still refused to live as if life were only Now.

Thus education can become both art and science. Someday soon we may quit our "problem" strategy: we may find that life is not a "problem" to be solved, but a picture to be painted, or, rather, that it is a pilgrimage to a shrine. The problem approach is the dubious bestowal of our scientific and mechanistic age: we look for some neat formula or some inventive gadget by which "to solve the problem" of life. We shall never find it. But if we see life as a pilgrimage, science also finds its place, and we can rejoice even in limitation. Football would be no fun without the white lines on a small field: imagine football played over a whole prairie! Music is fortunately held within its octave and within but a few pages of score: imagine an octave multiplied a hundredfold and a score as long as the books in the Congressional Library! Limitation is life—to those who know a world beyond the limits. Secular education has tried to build a keyboard ten miles long, and so has scurried up and down it like Gulliver on the piano of the giants,[27] and has hit it only here and there with a hammer too large to lift, and still has made no music. Faith can accept present bounds because it sees a larger dimension: life is not a problem to be solved, but a pilgrimage to a shrine. "Eye hath not seen, nor ear heard, neither have entered into the heart of man, the things which

God hath prepared for them that love him." [28] On that pilgrimage a man must journey in good will with his fellow pilgrims, for he and they must soon come to the shrine: "Thou shalt love the Lord thy God . . . and thy neighbour as thyself."

This assurance does not come by mind alone, but by the commitment of the whole man. If truth could be proved by the marshaling of facts and a resultant theorem, it would hardly be worth the proving. A wise preacher must again and again say to students' questions: "You are posing theoretical problems and seeking theoretical answers because you are living now in a thin academic light. Soon you will be married, and the children will come; and accidents will occur, and friends will be unbelievably kind; and then through sharp tragedy and devotion, through blundering and renewal, you will find your answer–because you will no longer trouble to ask this kind of question." All the more reason, therefore, why education should not be merely academic but a *collegium* bound in faith and friendship in the actual world! The student and professor, like Matthew Arnold's overworked preacher who saw no harvest of his labor in a London slum, but still fared bravely, also need

> a mark of everlasting light,
> Above the howling senses' ebb and flow
> To cheer thee, and to right thee if thou roam.[29]

Like that preacher, they need also the deed in the very streets lest the college be under stern judgment. We have seen hell in our time because men have lived by earthy standards—in business by the cult of things under man's mastery, in education by the cult of facts under man's supposedly sufficient mind. It would be an affront to any intelligent reader, now in our world of flaming judgment, to propose that hereafter there is no Judgment.

VI

By common knowledge students now ask "What's the use?"—or think it when it is not asked. The disillusionment is only brought to expression by the war and requirement of military service, for it is a disillusionment long-gathering as poison gas is long-gathering in a heavy swamp. The "What's the use?"—indeed the war itself—is only the final legacy. Students have been promised "the discovery of truth," but have found only half-truths taught by professors (strange title in our era!) who profess only relativities. They have heard airy talk of a still more airy "progress," but have found only war and the threat of planetary extinction. They, being young, could not themselves riddle our pretenses; and we could not help them, for we were ourselves deceived. So now students are tempted to brand all history as futility.

> Still we persist: plough the light sand, and sow
> Seed after seed where none can ever grow.[30]

It might be better if we *could* "persist," for we might then be kept from cruel mischief. But no man can long persist in that futility. So we snatch the passing day while hopes of an ampler life still vex us, or we turn violently on our neighbors because we secretly hate ourselves. Two communists told me bluntly: "Your Christianity may be true, but it is too slow." They had no world above this little world, so they must seize this world. They had no destination, so the accelerator and the clock were their only wisdom. They had no heaven, or could get there only on foot with fellow pilgrims, so they found it better to reach a slaughterhouse in a jet plane. Perhaps they are in part the product of a faithless education.

Our present flux calls the more urgently for faith's certitudes. Both politics and business are in transition, however entrenched minds may try to deny plain facts. Mass production has outrun mass power of purchase: momentous crux! The machine has become master instead of servant, and the soul has begun to rebel: portentous event! The common man everywhere is resolved, in motives not unmixed, to be rid once for all of the control which lately said to him, "Today you may work; tomorrow you may starve": end of an age! Life is once more in what the chemists call "solution," and the new precipitate has not yet appeared. Many of our seemingly impregnable systems have had "their day, and cease to be":[31] they are collapsing, if not from their own internal strains, then from time's erosion. Timid folk cry aloud that "we must go back," but there is no "back" in their sense of the word, for their once solid ground is itself in flux. Perhaps our generation must live in uncertainty. The more reason therefore, why it should not live in incertitude. The child lost in unaccustomed streets told the police: "If you will take me to the hill where the white cross stands, I can find my way."[32]

Education begins to question its own presumptions. The prophetic voices are still too few, but they no longer cry in a wilderness. Many a teacher who has been salt and savor to our common life welcomes their word. Many a teacher has longed for, and fulfilled in life if not in language, a better vocation than the dull expressionisms, factualisms, and methodologies for which faith has been foolishly bartered. This little book salutes such teachers. It confesses its own sin: the Church has also succumbed in some areas to a fictitious "progress" and the pride of man, and its failure has less excuse, for the Church should be the very home of faith. It joins hands with such teachers in greeting a new day. God has not yet done with us: Calvary did not daunt Him, much less thwart the outgoings of His love. There is need only to return to Him, in whom return is but a braver venture. To confess that the assumptions of recent education have been false is realism, the first step toward home. To avow once more the abiding implicits of the soul is to find home's welcome. "Thou shalt love the Lord thy God with all thy heart, and with all thy soul, and with all thy mind, and with all thy strength . . . and . . . thy neighbour as thyself."

REFERENCES

I. Person

1. Mark 12:28.
2. Mark 12:29-31; see also Matthew 22:37, 39; Luke 10:27.
3. James Bryant Conant, *Education in a Divided World* (Cambridge: Harvard University Press, 1948), p. 69.
4. John S. Brubacher, *Modern Philosophies of Education* (New York: McGraw-Hill Book Co., 1939), p. 329; also quoted by Edwin H. Rian, *Christianity and American Education* (San Antonio, Texas: The Naylor Co., 1949), p. 80.
5. *Educational Frontier,* ed. William H. Kilpatrick (Chicago: University of Chicago Press, 1933), pp. 72, 319; also quoted by Rian, *op. cit.*, p. 83.
6. George S. Counts, *Education and the Promise of America* (New York: The Macmillan Co., 1945), p. 148; also quoted by Rian, *op. cit.*, p. 83.
7. An example of this vagueness may be found in this typical sentence from John Dewey: "The needed unification can be obtained only as all subjects are organized with reference to their bearing upon the direction of social life." From *Education and the Social Order*, printed on the occasion of the John Dewey 90th Birthday Celebration (L.I.D. Pamphlet Series, League for Industrial Democracy, New York, 1936, reprinted 1949), p. 13.
8. Mary Coyle Chase in *Harvey* (New York: Dramatist Play Service, 1950).
9. John Dewey, *Education Today* (New York: G. P. Putnam's Sons, 1940), p. 3, as quoted by Rian, *op. cit.*, p. 81.
10. John Dewey, *A Common Faith* (New Haven: Yale University Press, 1934), p. 32.
11. *Ibid.*, p. 33.
12. A. N. Whitehead, *Science and the Modern World* (New York: The Macmillan Co., 1948), chap. 11, p. 257.
13. E. Griffith-Jones, *Faith and Verification* (London: Methuen & Co., Ltd., 1950), p. 19.
14. J. H. Woodger, *Biological Principles* (New York: Harcourt, Brace & Co., Inc., 1929), p. 228, has summarized and codified the assumptions of science. This passage is quoted with pungent comment by Arnold S. Nash, *The University and the Modern World* (New York: The Macmillan Co., 1943), pp. 95-96.
15. Romans 1:17; Galatians 3:11; Hebrews 10:38.

16. George Santayana, *Scepticism and Animal Faith* (New York: Charles Scribner's Sons, 1923), pp. 9-10.
17. Proverbs 4:18.
18. Milton, *Paradise Lost,* l. 543.
19. The word *eros* does not appear in the New Testament.
20. See John 15:13.
21. Told of Olive Schreiner. See S. C. Cronwright-Schreiner, *The Life of Olive Schreiner* (Boston: Little, Brown & Co., 1924), p. 67.
22. Walter Lippmann, *A Preface to Morals* (New York: The Macmillan Co., 1929), p. 113.
23. Tennyson, "The Ancient Sage."
24. Shakespeare, *King Lear,* Act V, scene 3.
25. London: SCM Press, Ltd., 56 Bloomsbury St., 1949.
26. Kenneth Scott Latourette, *The History of the Expansion of Christianity,* Vol. I, *The First Five Centuries* (New York: Harper & Bros., 1937), pp. 201-2; and see Webster's *Collegiate Dictionary* (5th ed.) under word "chapel."
27. Keats, "Ode to a Nightingale," st. vii.
28. H. Bence Jones, *The Life and Letters of Faraday* (London: Longmans, Green & Co., Ltd., 1870), I. 10.
29. John Masefield, "Biography," *Poems and Plays* (New York: The Macmillan Co., 1921).
30. John Morley, *The Life of William Ewart Gladstone* (New York: Macmillan & Co., 1903), I, 200.
31. Hebrews 9:26.

II. Community

1. Title of popular song written by J. Keirn Brennam; music by Ernest R. Ball.
2. Charles Mills Gayley, *Classic Myths* (Boston: Ginn & Co., 1893), pp. 220-21.
3. *Success Easier Than Failure* (Topeka, Kansas: Crane & Co., 1917), p. 52.
4. See Chap. I, p. 26.
5. Ephesians 4:32.
6. Luke 10:30-37.
7. Matthew 10:39.
8. In a little book called *Guesses at Truth* by two brothers, Julius Charles and Augustus William Hare, p. 436.
9. Essay entitled *Self-Reliance.*
10. See Charles Sanford Terry, *Bach; A Biography* (London: Oxford University Press, 1933), especially p. 70.
11. *Education and the Social Order,* p. 8.
12. Carl Sandburg, *Abraham Lincoln, the War Years* (New York: Harcourt, Brace & Co., Inc.), II, 404.
13. E.g., the Freudian claim to scientific truth, or his peremptory demand that every psychoanalyst should be psychoanalyzed, he himself as pioneer not having had the benefit! See *New Introductory Lectures on Psycho-*

anaylsis (New York: Norton & Co., 1933).

14. Title of a book by Miguel de Unamuno (London: The Macmillan Co., 1921).
15. New York: Harper & Bros., 1951.
16. For a penetrating discussion of this issue see Arnold S. Nash, *op. cit.*, part II.
17. *Education and the Social Order*, p. 8.
18. *Ibid.*, p. 10.
19. For interesting detail as well as probing thought see Henry P. Van Dusen, *God in Education* (New York: Charles Scribner's Sons, 1951), especially chap. 3; and Howard Lowry, *The Mind's Adventure* (Philadelphia: The Westminster Press, 1950), especially chaps. 3 and 4.
20. A personal experience where names would be a breach of confidence.
21. William Blake, "Auguries of Innocence."
22. *Ibid.*
23. Chap. 2.
24. *Short History of the English People.*
25. *Education for Responsible Living* (Cambridge: Harvard University Press, 1944), p. 32.
26. *Aims in Education* (New York: The Macmillan Co., 1929), p. 10.
27. Lewis Carroll, "The Walrus and the Carpenter," st. xi, from *Alice's Adventures Through the Looking Glass* (New York: Rand McNally & Co., 1916), chap. 4.
28. Gayley, *op. cit.*, p. 251.
29. II Corinthians 2:16.
30. I John 4:19.
31. I have not rediscovered the original source of this well-known quotation, but I find it also quoted in *A Treasury of Sermon Illustrations*, ed. Charles L. Wallis (New York and Nashville: Abingdon-Cokesbury Press, 1950), p. 48.
32. John Byrom, "Careless Content," *Poems* (printed for the Chetham Society, 1894), Vol. I, st. xi.
33. The hands are those of Franz Kingstien, lifetime friend of Dürer. See Cynthia Pearl Maus, *Christ and the Fine Arts* (New York: Harper & Bros., 1938), pp. 668-70.

III. Failure

1. *God and Evil* (New York: Harper and Brothers, 1943), p. 19.
2. Fred Clarke in *A Review of Educational Thought* (London: 1936), p. 25, as quoted by Arnold S. Nash, *op. cit.*, p. 273.
3. *Op. cit.*, pp. 54-55.
4. John 9:41 (R.S.V.).
5. Luke 22:53.
6. Milton, *Paradise Lost,* Bk. IV, l. 108.

7. *Mein Kampf* (New York: Stackpole Sons, 1939), pp. 111-12.
8. Romans 7:19.
9. *Liberalism and Social Action* (New York: G. P. Putnam's Sons, 1935), p. 82 and p. 52 as quoted, *op. cit.*, p. 120.
10. Psalm 138:8.
11. "Gold Hair."
12. *Ibid.*, sts. xxviii-xxx.
13. John 1:14.
14. Galatians 3:13.
15. I John 2:2.
16. Galatians 3:13.
17. Romans 13:10.
18. Luke 23:34.
19. Galatians 3:13.
20. Frederic W. H. Myers, *Saint Paul* (London: Macmillan & Co., 1928), p. 18.
21. Luke 2:29-30.
22. Mark 9:24.
23. See *College Teaching and Christian Values*, ed. Paul M. Limbert (New York: Association Press, 1951); Howard Lowry, *op. cit.*, particularly chap. 3; R. H. Edwin Espy, *The Religion of College Teachers* (New York: Association Press, 1951); Van Dusen, *op. cit.*, chap. 3.
24. Two useful books dealing in part with this subject are J. M. O'Neill, *Religion and Education Under the Constitution* (New York: Harper & Bros., 1949), and J. Paul Williams, *The New Education and Religion* (New York: Association Press, 1945).
25. In a statement made on "The Functions of Secondary Education in the United States" in *School and Society*, Vol. 72, No. 1866 (September 23, 1950), also quoted in *Information Service*, Federal Council of the Churches of Christ in America, Vol. XXIX, No. 36 (November 11, 1950).
26. In connection with the McCollum Case. See full account in O'Neill, *op. cit.*, chap. 12; and comments in Van Dusen, *op. cit.*, pp. 116-18.
27. *Op. cit.*, p. 70.
28. This phrase is from reading memory. I am sure it is from John Keats and is quoted in Amy Lowell, *John Keats* (Boston & New York: Houghton Mifflin Co., 1925), but I have not been able to rediscover the exact page.
29. Augustine, *The Confessions*, Bk. 1, sec. 1.
30. Shakespeare, *Macbeth*, Act I, scene 7.
31. Genesis 28:12.
32. Title of a play by Noel Coward; see *Play Parade* (Garden City, New York: Doubleday, Doran & Co., 1933).

IV. Destiny

1. Wallace Brett Donham (New York: McGraw-Hill Book Co., Inc., 1931).
2. Shelley, "Adonais," st. 52.

3. Based on II Peter 3:14 and Romans 11:33.
4. "A Grammarian's Funeral."
5. *The Republic*, especially Bks. VI and VII. The phrase "airy burgomasters" is a quotation from Milton, *Areopagitica.*
6. "A Grammarian's Funeral."
7. Milton, "Comus."
8. *Christian Doctrine* (Cambridge: The University Press, 1950), pp. 175-76.
9. "Oh May I Join the Choir Invisible," *The Complete Works of George Eliot* (Post Lethwaite, Taylor & Knowles, Ltd., 1908), I, 454.
10. I Corinthians 15:26 (R.S.V.).
11. II Timothy 1:10.
12. Hebrews 11:33.
13. I Corinthians 15:5-7.
14. Deuteronomy 21:23.
15. See Maurice Goguel, *The Life of Jesus* (New York: The Macmillan Co., 1933), chap. 1; Goguel, *Jesus the Nazarene* (New York: D. Appleton & Co., 1926), chap. 1, especially pp. 14-15; Albert Schweitzer, *The Quest of the Historical Jesus* (London: Adam & Charles Black, 1911); Chester Charlton McCown, *The Search for the Real Jesus* (New York, Charles Scribner's Sons, 1940).
16. I Corinthians 15:14-15.
17. II Timothy 1:10.
18. Acts 2:23-24 (R.S.V.).
19. Romans 5:20.
20. Luke 22:28.
21. "Thoughts Suggested on the Banks of the Nith."
22. William Allingham, "Blackberries."
23. I Corinthians 13:12 (my translation).
24. Title of book by John P. Marquand (Boston: Little, Brown & Co., 1943).
25. *The Republic*, Bk. 7, chap. 1.
26. See note 6.
27. Jonathan Swift, *Gulliver's Travels*, Pt. II, "A Voyage to Brobdingnag," chap. 6.
28. I Corinthians 2:9.
29. Sonnet, "East London."
30. Juvenal, *Satires* (William Gifford, trans.), st. vii, l. 48.
31. Tennyson, *In Memoriam*, prologue, st. 5.
32. Charles L. Wallis, *op. cit.*, p. 91, No. 691.